This book belongs to
YOU
of course . . .
who else?

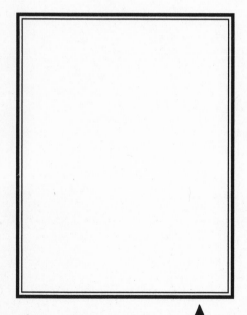

Self-portrait here ⌐
(You need to draw yourself.)

Lincoln Peirce

BiG NATE

BOREDOM BUSTER

DRAW LAUGH SCRIBBLE WRITE DRAW LAUGH SCRIBBLE WRITE

HARPER

An Imprint of HarperCollinsPublishers

BIG NATE is a registered trademark
of United Feature Syndicate, Inc.
The *Big Nate* comic strips appeared
in newspapers from January 25, 2008 to July 15, 2009.

ISBN 978-0-06-206094-5 (trade bdg.)
ISBN 978-0-06-209151-2 (Scholastic ed.)
ISBN 978-0-06-208993-9 (international ed.)

Typography by Andrea Vandergrift
11 12 13 14 15 CG/BV 10 9 8 7 6 5 4 3 2 1

First Edition

For Big Nate Fans Everywhere
Especially if you love—
Cheez Doodles,
Comics,
Fortune Cookies,
Doodling, and
Detention (Okay, forget that last one.)

SPOTLIGHT ON BIG NATE

Nate is awesome. Here's why.

Nate knows he's destined for greatness. Because he's no average 6th grader. He's meant for BIG things. He may not be Joe Honor Roll, but Nate's got many other more important talents.

THE MANY WAYS NATE SURPASSES ALL OTHERS:

Cartooning genius
(Specialty: teacher caricatures)

Soccer goalie

Table football star

Nickname czar of P.S. 38

WHAT DO YOU THINK IS SO GREAT ABOUT NATE?

1.

2.

3.

4.

5.

6.

7.

8. Cheez Doodle–eating champ

9.

10.

AND ... HERE'S
NATE'S BIGGEST
CLAIM TO FAME:
He is the <u>all-time record
holder</u> for detentions at
his school.

DOODLE DREAMS

Do you dream in doodles? Let loose and fill the page ALL OVER!

NATE'S TOP SECRET CODE

Nate is an ace at cracking codes. Maybe one day he'll become a super spy.

He invented a special code so he and his best buddies, Teddy and Francis, can send top secret messages for their eyes only—NOT for Nate's least favorite teacher, Mrs. Godfrey. Or for Gina, his Goody Two-shoes classmate, who always gets him into trouble!

CODE CHART Use this alphabet to decode the secret messages in this book!

Symbol	Letter	Symbol	Letter	Symbol	Letter	Symbol	Letter	Symbol	Letter	Symbol	Letter
								⊞ = U			
								⊟ = V			
⊡ =A	▯ = E	▽ =I	◖ = M	⊠ = Q	◎ = W						
⊖ =B	⊠ =F	◪ =J	◩ = N	⊞ = R	▨ = X						
◺ = C	⊻ = G	▣ = K	⊞ = O	⊡ = S	■ = Y						
◉ = D	⊟ =H	▬ =L	▮ = P	◈ =T	⊠ = Z						

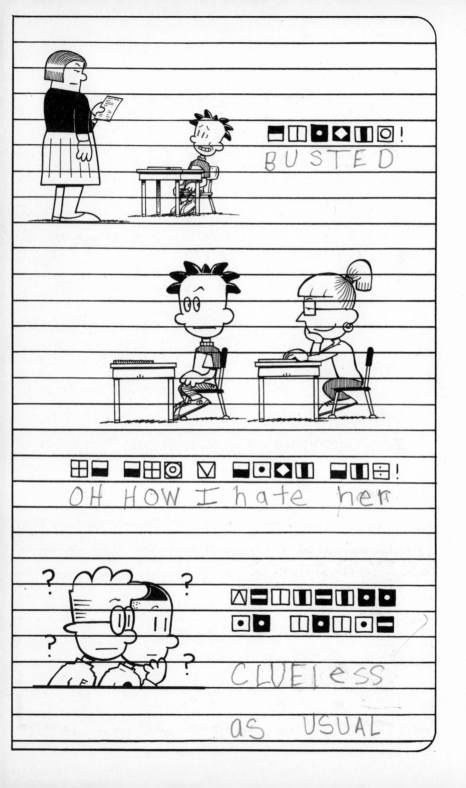

DETENTION ROOM

Watch out! Nate's in trouble AGAIN, with Godzilla . . . aka Mrs. Godfrey.

It's up to YOU to get him out of detention. Using the letters in the word "detention," how many other words can you make? If you find 15 words, Nate's free to play soccer with his best friends, Teddy and Francis! For a super challenge, find 25 words.

DETENTION

1.
2.
3.
4.
5.
6.
7. *dent*
8.
9.
10.
11.

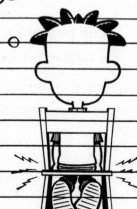

MY BUTT'S ASLEEP.

Act fast, or Nate might get stuck in detention . . . forever!

12.
13.
(Turn the page.)

DETENTION

14. _____
15. _____
16. _____
17. _____
18. _____
19. _____
20. _____
21. _____
22. _____
23. _____
24. _____
25. _____

**Congratulations! You have won the super
challenge. Now Nate gets to eat Cheez
Doodles every day for a week!**

INVENT-A-COMIX

Bring on the laughs! BIG time. Draw the funniest scene you can think of using Ben Franklin, volleyball, and Nate!

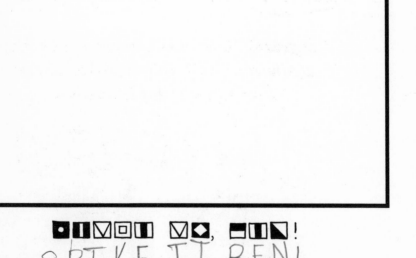

SPIKE IT, BEN!

CAST OF CHARACTERS

Nate's school, P.S. 38, may smell like mystery meat . . . ewww.

But it's also where Nate rules, and where you will find his best friends (#1 and #1A), his worst enemies, and his long-time crush—ever since 1st grade!

Can you name every character in Nate's world? Then decode the secret messages below them. Use the code chart on page 4.

Who are these characters?

France

Gina

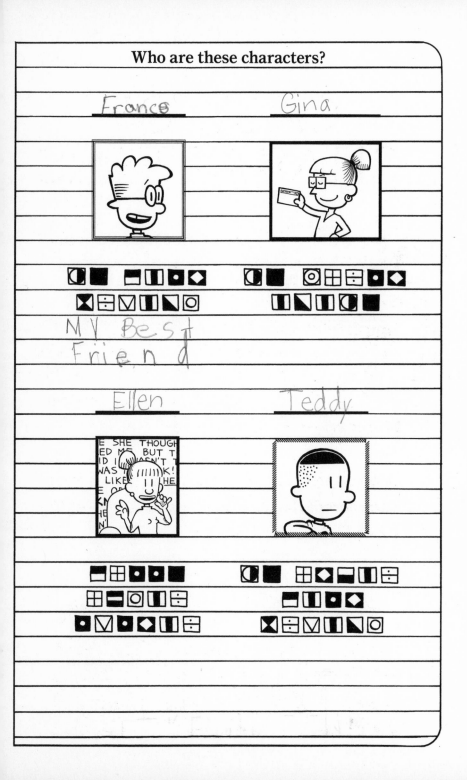

My Best
Friend

Ellen

Teddy

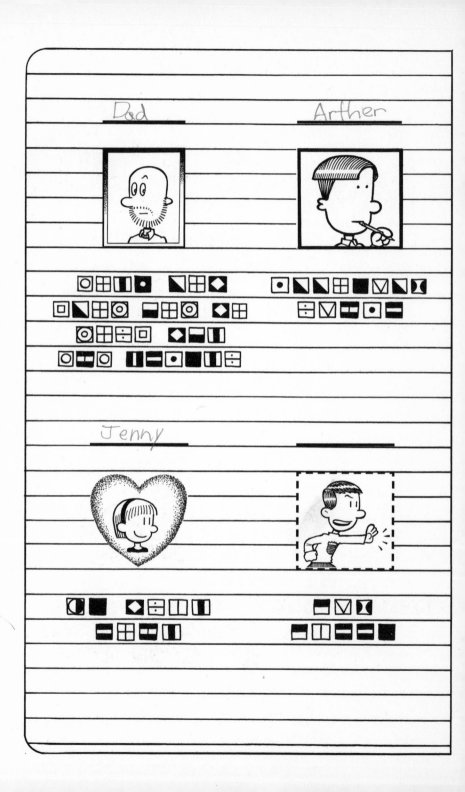

DeeDee

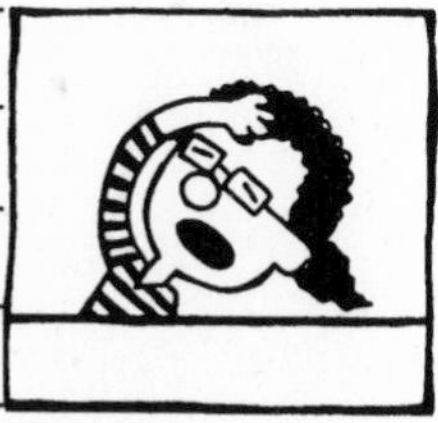

Spitsy

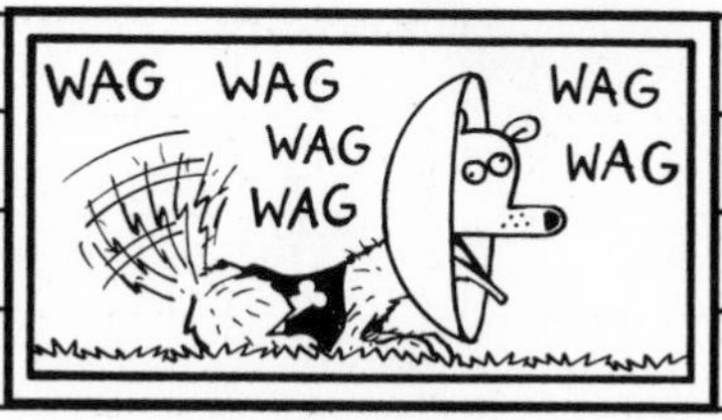

Chad

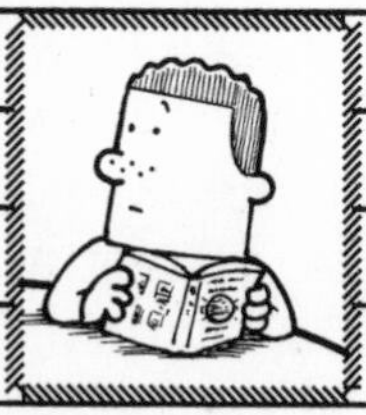

Sp

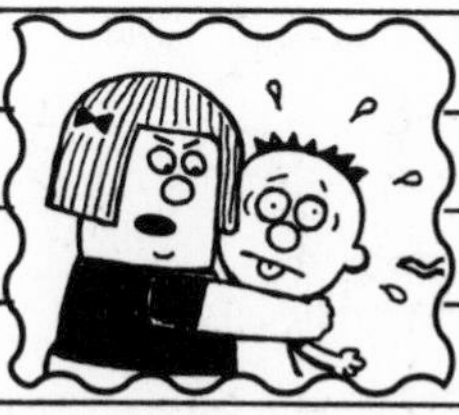

SUPER SCRIBBLE GAME

Nate plays the scribble game all the time. It's pretty simple: Somebody makes a scribble . . .

. . . and then you have to turn that scribble into a picture of something.

Fight boredom—start scribbling! Play the scribble game. Turn this scribble into something super cool.

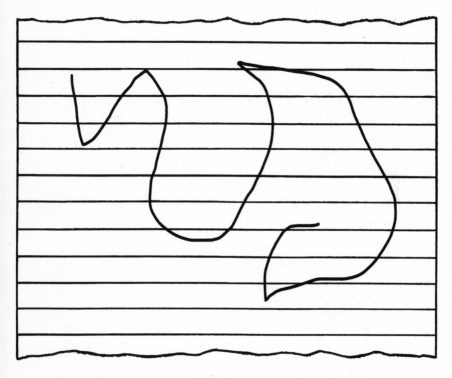

Don't forget to write a caption for it:

HEY, SPORTS FANS!
CHECK OUT BIG NATE'S

FLEECEBALL LINEUP

PAIGE

WILL

Nate doesn't get to choose his teammates. That's how Gina ends up on Nate's team.

TEDDY

SARAH

MARCIE

NATE

FRANCIS

COACH

CHAD

GINA

Here's your chance to create your own All-Star team. Who would you pick? Don't forget—YOU get to be captain.

DRAW YOURSELF HERE!

NATE'S WACKY WORLD

Quick! See if you can beat Nate!
Find all 22 words before he does.

ARTIST

ARTUR

CARTOONING

CHEEZ DOODLE

DETENTION

EGG SALAD

ELLEN

FLEECEBALL

FORTUNE

FRANCIS

GINA

GOALIE

GREATNESS

GREEN BEAN

HOMEWORK

JENNY

LOCKER

MR. ROSA

RANDY

SPITSY

SPOFF

TEDDY

```
A H I I M S P O F F O T K
N O T F R E K C O L O G R
I M H R R S I C N A R F Y
G E L D O O D Z E E H C E
N W N L S N A A A G A L Y
Z O F I A S J T C R L E D
N R O R P B N E T E T N N
R K R I N E E O N E O U A
A R T I S T O C I N D E R
E S U S T N Y K E B Y D O
Y O N O I T N E T E D W Y
F G E N O E G G S A L A D
N T G O A L I E F N R F D
```

POETRY SLAM: RHYME TIME

When inspiration strikes, it's time to write! The *Wright* way! Nate Wright, that is. Can you write an ode to your favorite snack?

ODE TO A CHEEZ DOODLE by Nate Wright

I search the grocery store in haste,

To find that sweet lip-smacking taste.

And there it is, in aisle nine.

It's just a dollar thirty-nine!

A bag of Doodles most delicious.

Check the label: They're nutritious!

And do you know how satisfied

I feel while munching Doodles fried?

I savor each bright orange curl,

Until it seems I just might hurl.

Their praises I will always sing.

Cheez Doodles are my everything.

Is it ice cream? Or pizza? Or Cheez Doodles, Nate's true love? What makes YOU drool with hunger? Write it here: _____

Make a list of words that describe or are related to your yummy treat.

Example: pizza (crispy, cheese, cheesy, pepperoni, crust, sauce, bubbly, gooey)

POETRY! PORTFOLIO!
Nate Wright

You can be a poet, too. Put your skills to the test!
Here are some words that rhyme with **funny:**
sunny, money, honey

Now you try! Come up with words that rhyme
with **Nate: great, late, wait** _____

_____

Tree: bee, sea, me, glee
Come up with five more! _____

_____

Rain: mane, lane, drain, cane
List six more! _____

_____

Now try these:
Crash _____
Hot _____
Spit _____
Game _____
Mind _____

Now try writing couplets (that's
two lines that rhyme).

MANY   JENNY
PENNY   ANY

☺ Some say ketchup is not a food
Well, I say they are really rude.

☺ When I feel a rumble in my tummy,
I search frantically for something _____.

☺ Nothing in the world is more special to me
Than syrup from a maple _____ !

☺ When a bag of marshmallows is near,
You can see me grinning from ear to _____.

Write your own couplets here:

Now you are ready to write an ode. Remember, the last word in each line of a couplet has to rhyme.

ODE TO _____

■⊞❒ •⊡❙❒ • ❙⊞❙◆ •◥◐

■⊞❒ ◐▽◐ ◥⊞◆ ◐◥⊞◐ ▽◆.

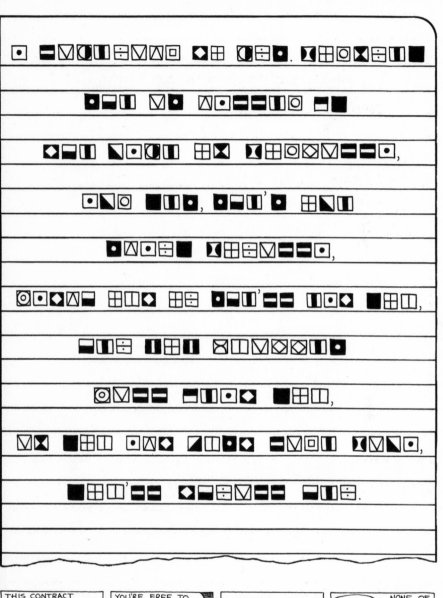

THIS CONTRACT REQUIRES YOU TO READ ONE BOOK PER WEEK FOR THE REST OF THE SUMMER.

SIGH...

YOU'RE FREE TO CHOOSE FROM ANY OF THESE TITLES.

WHA-? YOU MADE A LIST?

WAIT A MINUTE! I'VE NEVER HEARD OF ANY OF THESE BOOKS!

YOU'RE CATCHING ON.

NONE OF THESE ARE POETRY, ARE THEY? I DON'T DO POETRY UNLESS IT'S LIMERICKS.

© 2009 by NEA, Inc.

WORST DAYS EVER!

Even though Nate is awesome, things don't always go his way. He's had his share of bad days. Like the time his dad showed up for middle school skating night wearing FIGURE SKATES. Or the Spring Fever dance, when Jenny and Artur became a couple.

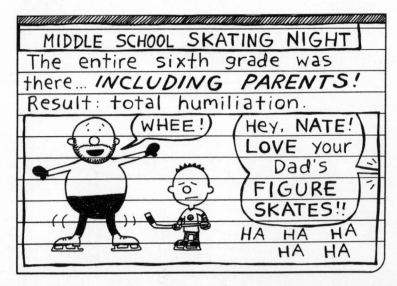

MIDDLE SCHOOL SKATING NIGHT
The entire sixth grade was there... *INCLUDING PARENTS!*
Result: total humiliation.

WHEE!

Hey, NATE! LOVE your Dad's FIGURE SKATES!!

HA HA HA HA HA

Have you ever had a bad day? What if your list of WORST DAYS EVER looked like this? Would you rank them as BAD, AWFUL, or WORST?

WORST DAYS EVER

1. On your way to a birthday party, a bird poops on you.

☐ BAD   ☐ AWFUL   ☐ WORST

2. On picture day, you spill ketchup on your sweater.

☐ BAD   ☐ AWFUL   ☐ WORST

3. Your teacher gives you a pop quiz.

☐ BAD   ☐ AWFUL   ☐ WORST

4. You wear your shirt backward to school.

☐ BAD   ☐ AWFUL   ☐ WORST

5. You lose your lucky charm.

☐ BAD   ☐ AWFUL   ☐ WORST

6. Everyone thinks you wet your pants.

☐ BAD   ☐ AWFUL   ☐ WORST

7. You forgot to do all your homework.

☐ BAD   ☐ AWFUL   ☐ WORST

8. You throw up in front of your crush.

☐ BAD   ☐ AWFUL   ☐ WORST

9. Your best friend moves away.

☐ BAD   ☐ AWFUL   ☐ WORST

10. Your sister ate all the Cheez Doodles.

☐ BAD   ☐ AWFUL   ☐ WORST

11. You just got detention.

☐ BAD   ☐ AWFUL   ☐ WORST

POP QUIZ!

Nate's never been the teacher's pet. That's
because he's too busy being the class clown!
Can you name Nate's teachers?
Match the teachers to the class they teach.

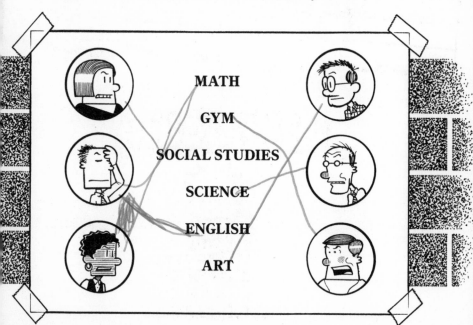

MATH

GYM

SOCIAL STUDIES

SCIENCE

ENGLISH

ART

QUESTION OF THE DAY:

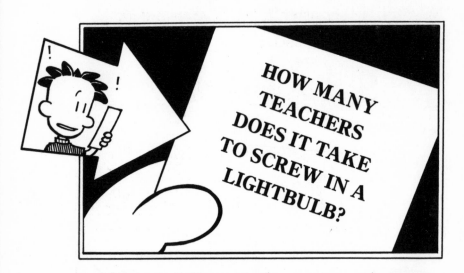

HOW MANY TEACHERS DOES IT TAKE TO SCREW IN A LIGHTBULB?

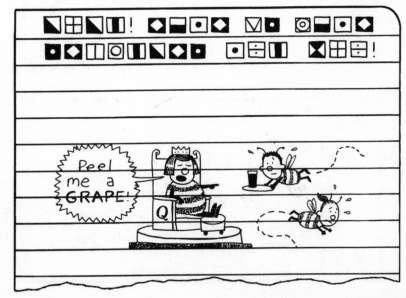

COOL COMIX!

Nate's bossy big sister, Ellen, is annoying him . . . again! Fill in the speech bubbles and help him get his revenge.

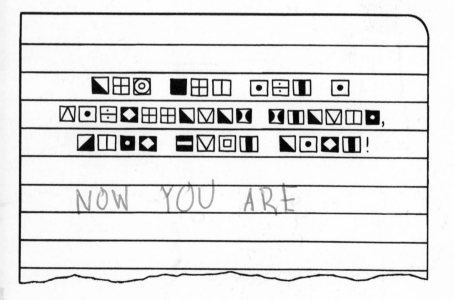

NOW YOU ARE

BEST BUDS

Nate, Teddy, Francis, and Spitsy love to hang out. Make sure they're all together! Can you figure out who should go where so that each character appears only once in every row, column, and box of four squares?

N = **NATE**

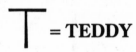

F = **FRANCIS**

T = **TEDDY**

S = **SPITSY**

NICKNAME CZAR

Nate gets called a lot of things . . . like . . .

Actually, Nate is the master of inventing nick-names for other people, like his scary social studies teacher, Mrs. Godfrey. Help Nate come up with the rest of his list. Now you are a nickname czar, just like Nate!

CHECK
MY LIST!

GODFREY NICKNAMES

1. Godzilla
2. Boring.com
3.
4.
5.
6.
7.
8.
9.
10.
11.
12.
13.
14.
15.
16.

FRANCIS'S FANTASTIC SECRET ALPHABET

Francis is seriously smart! He's such a brainiac that Nate's always spying on him to find out what homework they have. It's payback time! Francis is going to fool Nate in a BIG way. He's invented a secret alphabet that Nate will never decode!

WHAT ARE YOU WRITING?

Use the alphabet to translate Francis's message to you. Don't tell Nate! You're <u>undercover</u>.

A	B	C	D	E	F	G	H	I	J	K	L	M
13	7	26	25	8	16	3	1	20	4	12	23	18

N	O	P	Q	R	S	T	U	V	W	X	Y	Z
21	11	2	15	14	24	6	10	19	22	17	9	5

H M M M M.

$\overline{20}\ \overline{21}$ $\overline{7}\ \overline{20}\ \overline{3}$ $\overline{21}\ \overline{13}\ \overline{6}\ \overline{8}$

$\overline{11}\ \overline{21}$ $\overline{13}$ $\overline{14}\ \overline{11}\ \overline{23}\ \overline{23}$,

$\overline{23}\ \overline{11}\ \overline{11}\ \overline{12}$ $\overline{11}\ \overline{10}\ \overline{6}$ $\overline{16}\ \overline{11}\ \overline{14}$

$\overline{2}\ \overline{8}\ \overline{6}\ \overline{8}\ \overline{14}$ $\overline{2}\ \overline{13}\ \overline{21}$,

$\overline{6}\ \overline{20}\ \overline{18}\ \overline{7}\ \overline{8}\ \overline{14}$ $\overline{24}\ \overline{26}\ \overline{11}\ \overline{10}\ \overline{6}\ \overline{24}$,

$\overline{13}\ \overline{21}\ \overline{25}$ $\overline{25}\ \overline{8}\ \overline{6}\ \overline{8}\ \overline{21}\ \overline{6}\ \overline{20}\ \overline{11}\ \overline{21}$,

$\overline{11}\ \overline{16}$ $\overline{26}\ \overline{11}\ \overline{10}\ \overline{14}\ \overline{24}\ \overline{8}$.

SUPERHERO POWERS

IF YOU WERE A SUPERHERO, WHAT AMAZING POWERS WOULD YOU HAVE?

Circle your top 5!

Walking on Water	
X-ray Vision	
Flight	
Super Speed	
Shape-Shifting	
Power Hearing	
Thought Control	
Anti-Aging	
Cloning	
Shrinking	
Fireproof	
Time Travel	

Super Jumping

Weather Master

Scaling Tall Buildings

Mind Reading

Breathing Underwater

Invisibility

Anti-Gravity

Force Field Generator

Magnetism

CAN YOU THINK OF ANY
OTHER SUPERPOWERS?
ADD THEM HERE:

WHAT DOES YOUR SUPERHERO DO?

SHOW YOUR SUPERHERO:

SCALING TALL BUILDINGS

CLONING

SHAPE-SHIFTING

WALKING ON WATER

Does your superhero save the day?
Make your own comix.
Your name here

IN THE CAFETORIUM

Which foods gross you out? See if you can solve this crossword and name all the foods that make Nate and his friends gag!

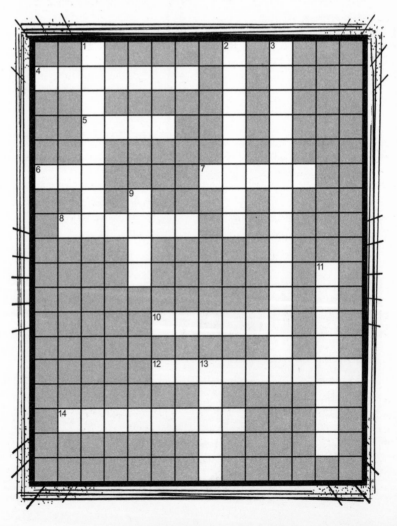

CLUES

ACROSS

4. It's leafy, green, and Popeye eats it to grow strong!

5. Chickens lay these.

6. Split ___ soup.

7. Rhymes with "shiver" and served with onions.

8. Healthy, stringy, and light green. WAY better with peanut butter.

10. Red, round, and rhymes with potato.

12. First word rhymes with "dish," and swims. Second word rhymes with "kick."

14. First word is the same as a city in Peru. Often found on the dinner plate—eww.

DOWN

1. This crispy snack looks like Styrofoam. Nate's dad gave them out for Halloween—ugh!

2. Smelly, comes from the sea. Your mom likes to mix it with mayonnaise for sandwiches.

3. Round, small, and green, and looks like a little cabbage. Yuck!

9. Rhymes with "feet." Dark red and slimy.

11. Looks like a mini tree. Nate's dad serves it with cheese sauce. Gross.

13. Lives in a shell. If you were French, you'd gobble it up.

THE CHAMP

Nate is the CHAMP! Solve the maze so there can be a SPOFFY in his future.

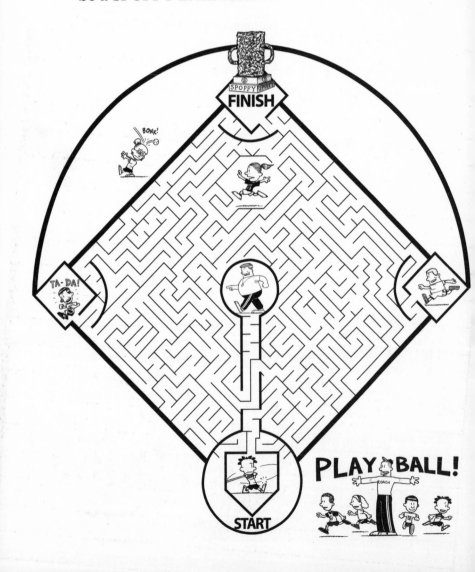

PERSONALITY POP QUIZ

WHICH BIG NATE CHARACTER ARE YOU MOST LIKE?

1. What is the snack you eat most often?

   a. Granola bar

   b. An apple

   c. Chinese food

   d. Cheez Doodles

   e. Chocolate

2. Your favorite school subject is:

   a. Social studies

   b. All of them!

   c. Gym

   d. Art

   e. English

3. What is your favorite after school activity?

    a. Student council

    b. Studying

    c. Baseball

    d. Drawing comix

    e. Drama club

4. Your favorite teacher is:

    a. Mrs. Godfrey

    b. Mr. Staples

    c. Coach

    d. Mr. Rosa

    e. Ms. Clarke

5. Kids in your class might say that you are a

    a. Teacher's pet

    b. Braniac/nerd

    c. Jock

    d. Class clown

    e. Drama queen

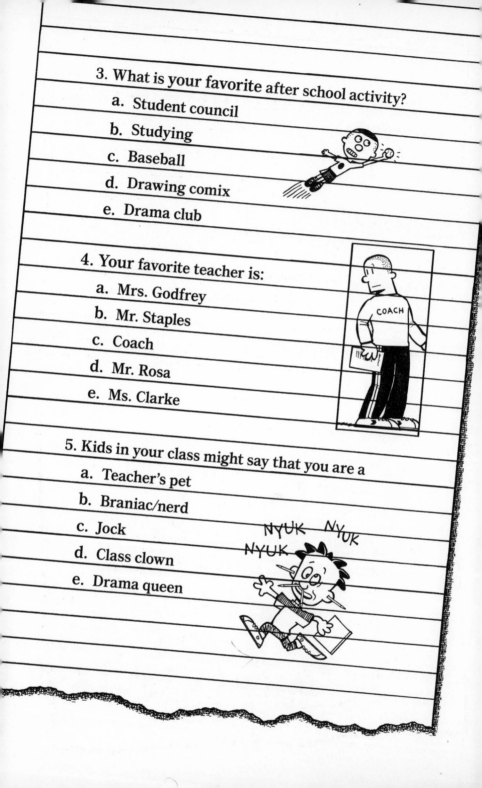

*If you answered A the most times, you're a lot like Gina.

B = Francis

C = Teddy

D = Nate

E = Ellen

SUPER SCRIBBLE GAME

What can you turn
this scribble into?

Write your caption here:

DAD IS NOT
A BLAST

DAD FACTS:

1. Nate's dad has been known to wear figure skates.   T   F

2. Nate's dad always has potato chips in the house.   T   F

3. Nate's dad gave out rice cakes for Halloween once.   (T)   F

4. Nate's dad is best friends with Gina's dad.   (T)   F

GENIUS

Even though Nate is a self-described genius, he does NOT plan on achieving greatness in:

Synchronized swimming

Opera

Writing a health food cookbook

CAT GROOMING

What about you? Circle all that apply!

I WON'T ACHIEVE GREATNESS IN . . .

Counting paper clips

Fly swatting

Speed blinking

Color-coding my sock collection

Candlemaking

Underwater basket weaving

WHAT ELSE?

LIST YOUR NON-GOALS HERE!

SUPERHERO COMIX

Nate created his very own superhero... Ultra-Nate.

DRAW YOURSELF AS A SUPERHERO!

CHEEZ DOODLE ALERT

Nate needs Cheez Doodles.
Help him get to them, pronto!

ANOTHER TEST!

DO YOU THINK THESE STATEMENTS ARE TRUE OR FALSE?

1. Nate's never been to detention.
   ☐ TRUE   ☐ FALSE

2. The earth goes around the sun.
   ☐ TRUE   ☐ FALSE

3. Jenny has always loved Nate.
   ☐ TRUE   ☐ FALSE

4. Ben Franklin got an A in 7th grade science.
   ☐ TRUE   ☐ FALSE

5. Nate's neighbor's dog, Spitsy, eats his own poop.
   ☐ TRUE   ☐ FALSE

6. "Enslave the Mollusk" is the name of Nate's band.
   ☐ TRUE   ☐ FALSE

IF YOU DO THIS POORLY ON THE **NEXT** TEST, NATE, YOU COULD VERY WELL END UP IN SUMMER SCHOOL!

7. Pluto is a planet.

    □ TRUE   □ FALSE

8. Nate once ran through gym class with his shorts
filled with green Jell-O.

    □ TRUE   □ FALSE

9. Green beans are Nate's favorite snack.

    □ TRUE   □ FALSE

10. Nate's big sister, Ellen, was in Mrs. Godfrey's class.

    □ TRUE   □ FALSE

EXTRA CREDIT

11. "Epidermis" is another word for skin.

    □ TRUE   □ FALSE

EXTRA EXTRA CREDIT

12. Gina once sang a duet with Nate.

    □ TRUE   □ FALSE

TEDDY'S TOP SECRET CODE

Teddy is a sports nut. He collects sports facts and sends them to Nate. Using Teddy's secret code, help Nate decipher Teddy's amazing sports trivia.

A	B	C	D	E	F	G	H	I	J	K	L	M
Z	Y	X	W	V	U	T	S	R	Q	P	O	N

N	O	P	Q	R	S	T	U	V	W	X	Y	Z
M	L	K	J	I	H	G	F	E	D	C	B	A

<u>A</u> <u>l</u> <u>l</u>   <u>M</u> <u>L</u> <u>B</u>   <u>U</u> <u>M</u> <u>P</u> <u>I</u> <u>R</u> <u>E</u> <u>S</u>
Z O O   N O Y   F N K R I V H

<u>M</u> <u>U</u> <u>S</u> <u>T</u>   <u>W</u> <u>E</u> <u>A</u> <u>R</u>   <u>B</u> <u>L</u> <u>A</u> <u>C</u> <u>K</u>
N F H G   D V Z I   Y O Z X P

<u>U</u> <u>N</u> <u>D</u> <u>E</u> <u>R</u> <u>W</u> <u>E</u> <u>A</u> <u>R</u>   <u>w</u> <u>h</u> <u>i</u> <u>l</u> <u>e</u>
F M W V I D V Z I   D S R O V

<u>O</u> <u>N</u>   <u>t</u> <u>h</u> <u>e</u>   <u>J</u> <u>o</u> <u>b</u>!
L M   G S V   Q L Y

<u>T</u> <u>h</u> <u>e</u>   __ __ __   __ __ __ __ __ __ __
G S V   G Z O O V H G

__ __ __ __ __ __ __   __ __   __ __ __
K O Z B V I   R M   G S V

__ __ __   __ __   __ __ __ __ __ __ __ __ __
M Y Z   R H   X F I I V M G O B

__ __ __   __ __ __ __.
B Z L   N R M T

__ __   __ __
S V   R H

__ __ __ __ __   __ __ __ __'
H V E V M   U V V G

__ __ __   __ __ __ __ __ __ __.
H R C   R M X S V H

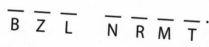

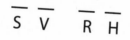

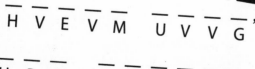

IT'S CRAZY IN 3010!

In Nate's Cool Comix, Ben Franklin travels from the 1700s to the 21st century in his very own time machine! If you could travel to the future, what would you find there? Use the following steps to create your time travel adventure!

First, let's review. What is a noun?

OOH! A noun is a person, place, or thing.

EXAMPLES: Nate (person), P.S. 38 (place), report card (thing)

What is a verb?

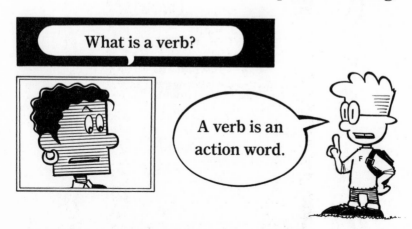

A verb is an action word.

EXAMPLES: study, laugh, play, calculate

Nate, what is an adjective?

SAY WHAT?

BING!

An adjective is a word that describes a noun.
Some examples of adjectives are:
AWESOME (describes me)
BORING (describes social studies)
CRAZY (describes Doctor Cesspool)

AND, an adverb is a word that describes a verb. Here's how to use one in a sentence: Gina behaves obnoxiously.

MAKE A LIST OF THE SILLIEST WORDS YOU CAN THINK OF:

1. Noun:

2. Noun:

3. Noun (plural):

4. Noun (plural):

5. Noun (plural):

6. Adjective:

7. Adjective:

8. Adjective:

9. Adjective:

10. Noun (plural):

11. Noun (plural):

12. Verb:

13. Verb:

14. Adjective:

ANYBODY GOT A TISSUE?

NOW TURN THE PAGE AND USE YOUR LIST
TO FILL IN THE BLANKS!

THE FUTURE IS WILL!

IMAGINE YOUR TIME TRAVEL MACHINE
LANDED IN 3010 . . .

· I've just arrived in the city __Zyrwc__ on the planet __Mars__, where there are lots of funny-looking __elf__ that breathe __carrots__ and like to eat __Iphone__. The sky is __green__ and the water is __orange__. The people are __short__ and __fat__. They fly these tiny __shoes__ and sleep on __tables__. They __fart__ and __burp__ at me instead of saying hi. What a __crazy__ place!

_____

_____

DRAW-A-THON

Nate's favorite class in school is art . . . it's gotta be the ONE place where Nate hasn't gotten a detention slip!

OOPS!

Never mind.

Dare to draw! Are you an artist like Nate? Or his rival, Artur? Take off your shoe and draw it!

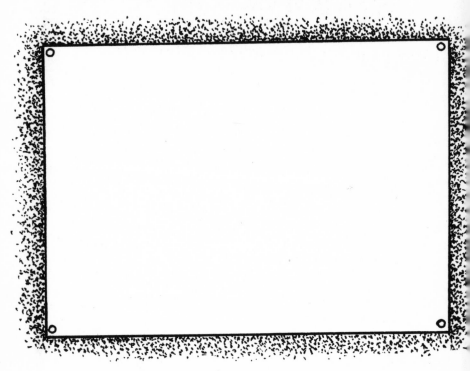

CHECK OUT ARTUR'S DRAWING!

"OLD SHOE" BY ARTUR

TEACHER
TROUBLE

Find out which teachers gave Nate detention today! Fill in the blanks so each teacher appears only once in every row, column, and box.

 G = **MRS. GODFREY**

 **C** = **COACH JOHN**

 P = **PRINCIPAL NICHOLS**

 **S** = **MR. STAPLES**

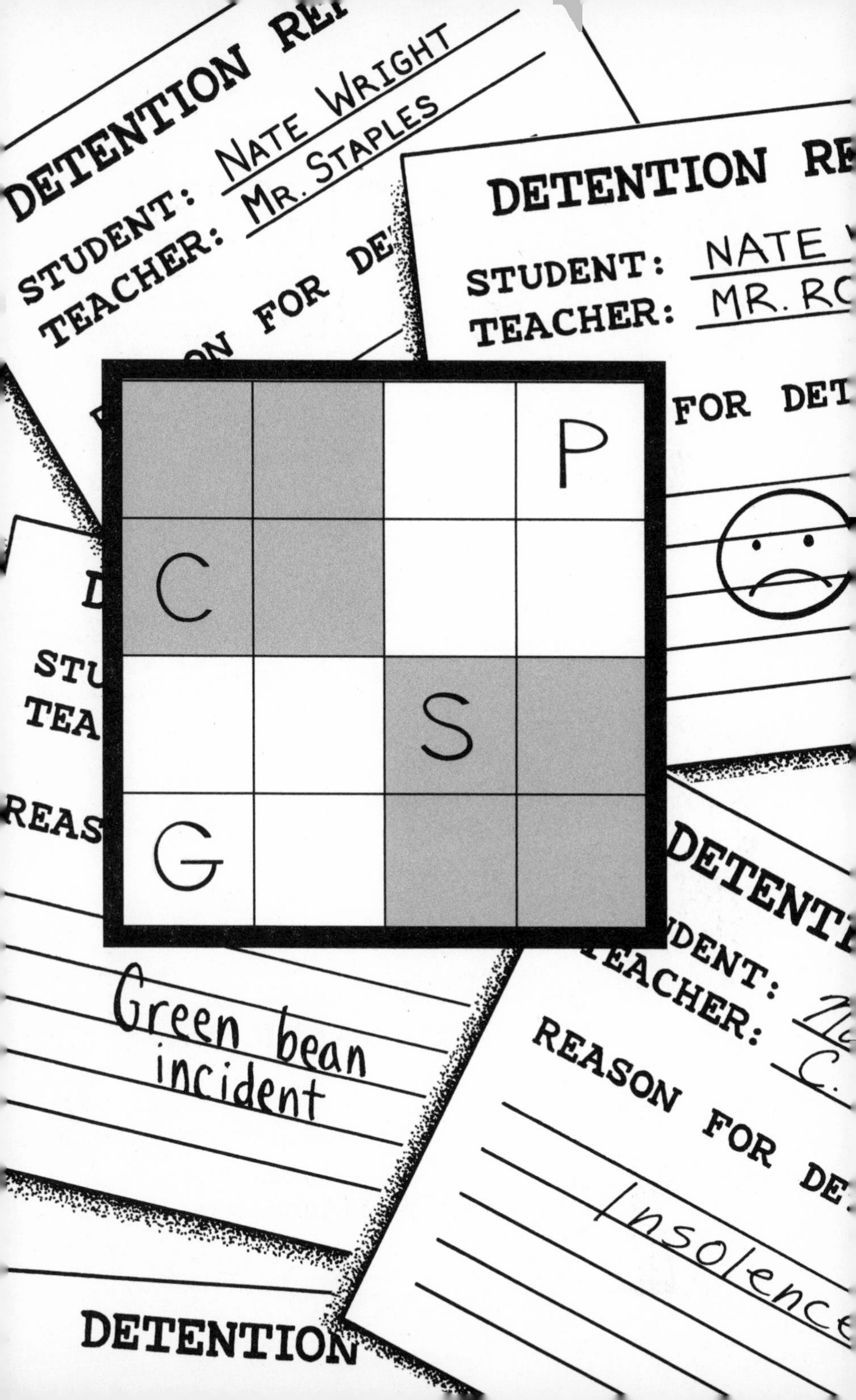

DETENTION
STUDENT: NATE WRIGHT
TEACHER: MR. STAPLES
FOR
DETENTION
STUDENT: NATE
TEACHER: MR.
FOR
P
C
S
G
Green bean incident
TEACHER:
REASON FOR
Insolence
DETENTION

COSMIC COOKIES

Nate is superstitious. When he eats at Pu Pu Panda, he always gets a fortune cookie. Help him decode all of his fortunes.

CRUNCH CRUNCH

PLUS, THE COOKIES TASTE LIKE STYROFOAM.

_____

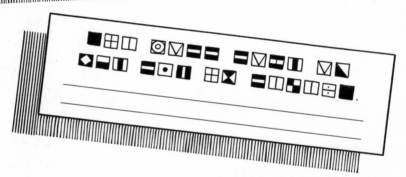

_____

H M M M M...

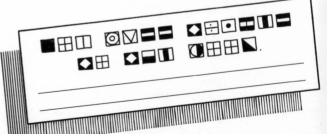

_____

Crack open a cookie . . . what would you want your fortune to be?

A large life is a series of small events.

Today you will surpass all others.

Hair today, gone tomorrow.

Some fortunes are so mysterious . . .

. . . they make no sense at all!

Make up the wackiest and weirdest fortunes ever.

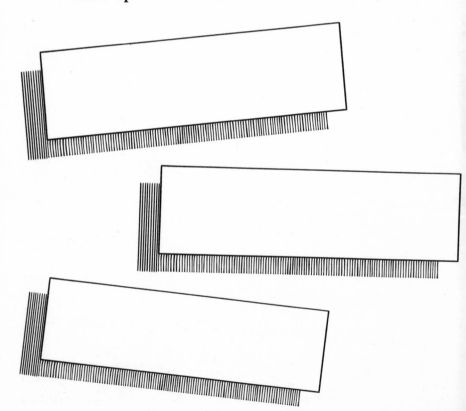

WEIRD BUT TRUE

Use Francis's undercover alphabet on page 39 to decode!

$\overline{}$ $\overline{6}$ $\overline{1}$ $\overline{8}$ $\overline{6}$ $\overline{20}$ $\overline{6}$ $\overline{13}$ $\overline{21}$

$\overline{7}$ $\overline{8}$ $\overline{8}$ $\overline{6}$ $\overline{23}$ $\overline{8}$ $\overline{26}$ $\overline{13}$ $\overline{21}$ $\overline{3}$ $\overline{14}$ $\overline{11}$ $\overline{22}$

$\overline{10}$ $\overline{2}$ $\overline{6}$ $\overline{11}$ $\overline{8}$ $\overline{20}$ $\overline{3}$ $\overline{1}$ $\overline{6}$

$\overline{20}$ $\overline{21}$ $\overline{26}$ $\overline{1}$ $\overline{8}$ $\overline{24}$ $\overline{20}$ $\overline{21}$ $\overline{23}$ $\overline{8}$ $\overline{21}$ $\overline{3}$ $\overline{6}$ $\overline{1}$.

I'M DOING WHAT YOU DID! I'M POSTING A LIST OF 25 RANDOM THINGS ABOUT MYSELF!

...BUT UNLIKE **YOU**, I'M GOING TO STICK TO THE **FACTS**! EVERYTHING ON **MY** LIST IS GOING TO BE 100% **TRUE**!

1.) I like oatmeal.

TIK TIK TIK TAK

TRUTH ONE, EXCITEMENT ZERO.

2.) I like to put raisins in my oatmeal.

ÜBER-AWESOME WAY-OUT NAME-A-THON

Mix and match these words to make your own wacky names!

Pepperoni

Poodle

Stinky

Egg salad

Secret

Funky

Turbospeed

Brainiac

Royal

Giant

Crazy

Cheese

Horse

Spittle

Squid

Green bean

Slinky

Dorkosaurus

Porcupine

Dancing

Head

King

Noogie

Machine

Cookie

Star

Champion

Hair

Princess

Genius

HERE ARE SOME VERY SILLY NAMES:

Stinky Cheese Head

Noogie Poodle

Green Bean Funky Hair

NOW CREATE YOUR OWN!

_____ _____ _____

_____ _____

_____ _____ _____

_____ _____ _____

_____ _____

_____ _____

_____ _____ _____

_____ _____

_____ _____ _____

_____ _____ _____

_____ _____ _____

_____ _____

EXTRA! EXTRA!

Nate writes for the school newspaper. You can, too!
What do you see in each picture? Fill in the caption!

SUPER SCRIBBLE GAME

Guess what? It's time for the scribble game!

Don't forget to write a caption for your scribble!

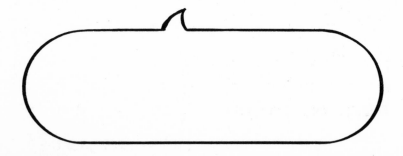

VACATION
IS BEST!

Do you love summer vacation as much as Nate?

No teachers! No books!

HOW I SPENT MY SUMMER VACATION!
by: Nate Wright

The **BEST** time I had all summer was when Francis invited me to his grandparents' cabin on Echo Lake. I learned two things: 1.) water skiing is fun, and 2.) wiping out is a **BLAST!!**

WA-HOOO!

Then the 4th of July Fair came to town. There were some new rides this year, and they **ROCKED!**

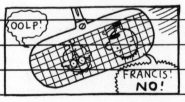

OOLP!

FRANCIS! NO!

LIST YOUR TOP 10 SUMMER FUN TIMES:

1.

2.

3.

4.

5.

6.

7.

8.

9.

10.

I WANT YOU TO SIGN THIS CONTRACT PROMISING TO READ SOME BOOKS THIS SUMMER.

A CONTRACT? YOU'RE FORCING ME TO READ?

I DON'T WANT TO READ BECAUSE YOU'RE **MAKING** ME READ! I WANT TO READ FOR THE SHEER **JOY** OF IT!

UH-HUH. AND HOW OFTEN DO YOU READ FOR THE SHEER JOY OF IT?

ALL THE **TIME**!

...NOT INCLUDING COMIC BOOKS.

OH. THEN NEVER.

CRAZY COMIX!

What is that wacky doctor up to? You decide.
Write your own speech bubbles.

DOCTOR CESSPOOL!

TRASHED!

Randy has a date . . . with a coconut yogurt pie.

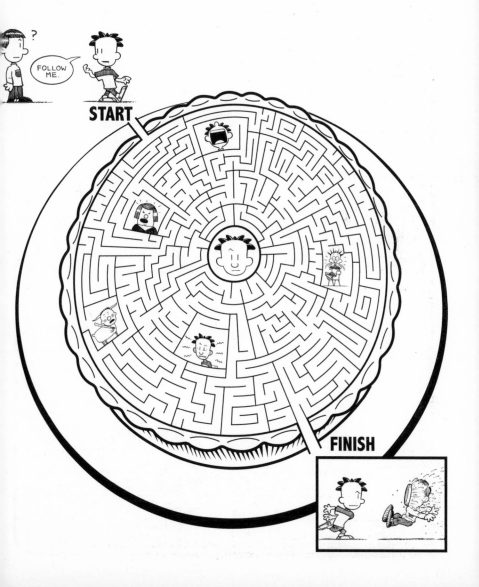

KNOCKOUT KNOCK-KNOCK JOKES

Nate's math teacher, Mr. Staples, loves to tell corny knock-knock jokes. Anything's more fun than math, right? Try his jokes out on your friends!

Knock knock!

Who's there?

Ice cream!

Ice cream who?

Ice cream if you don't let me in!

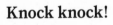

Knock knock!

Who's there?

A little old lady.

A little old lady who?

I didn't know you could yodel.

MAKE YOUR OWN KNOCKOUT
KNOCK-KNOCK JOKES!

Knock knock!

Who's there?

Ketchup!

Ketchup who?

Ketchup to me and I'll tell you.

Knock knock!

Who's there?

Police!

_____ who?

Police _____.

Knock knock!

_____ ?

Water!

_____ who?

Water _____.

CLAPPA CLAP CLAP

Knock knock!

_____ ?

_____ !

_____ who?

_____.

NATE CAN'T ☹ STAND IT! ☹

These are the things that get under Nate's skin.
Help him rank them from #1 to #10.

School picture day

Being sick during the weekend

cats

"Oldies" music

Gina

Paper cuts

SNORT!

Egg salad

Social studies

Bubble gum that loses its flavor in twenty seconds

Figure skating

THINGS I CAN'T STAND!

by:  ← Nate Wright, esq.

1.

2.

3.

4.

5.

6.

7.

8.

9.

10.

WHAT'D YOU GET ON THE TEST, EINSTEIN?

NONE OF YOUR BUSINESS, GINA!

WELL, WITH THE EXTRA CREDIT, I GOT A PERFECT SCORE: 105!

105 ISN'T A PERFECT SCORE.

WHA-... WHAT?

THERE WERE SIX EXTRA CREDIT POINTS! I GOT A 106!

BUT!... ✳SPLUTTER!✳... ✳SPLUT!✳...I...

HEY, GINA! DOES SHE REMIND YOU OF ANYBODY?

THE GANG'S ALL HERE!

It's a BIG NATE reunion! Fill in the blanks so each of your favorite (or LEAST favorite) BIG NATE characters appear only once in every row, column, and box.

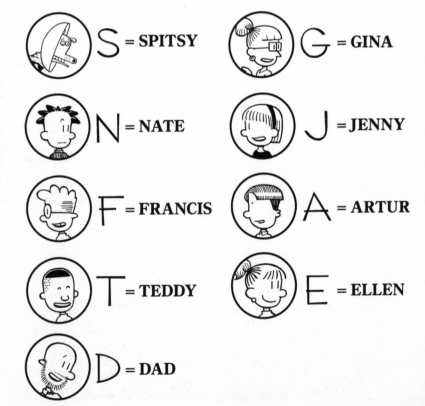

S = SPITSY

N = NATE

F = FRANCIS

T = TEDDY

D = DAD

G = GINA

J = JENNY

A = ARTUR

E = ELLEN

S	G		N		F	J	
F	T	J		G		A	D
	A		F	J	D	S	G
	J				D	N	
T	E	S	N	D	J		G
	G	N		A		T	E
E			G	A	J		N
G	N	D	J	S		F	A
	F		E			S	T

COMIX BY U!

Unleash the cartoonist in you! Make your own comic using Gina, Nate, and his locker.

?

YOUR TITLE HERE

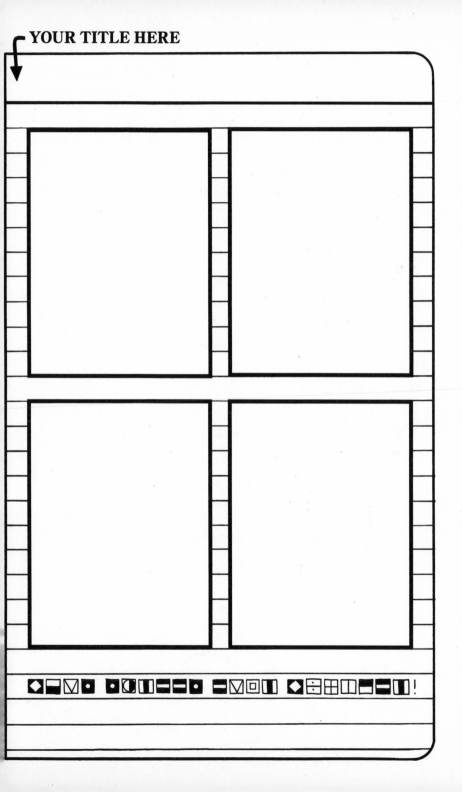

TOP JOKESTER

According to Teddy, the lamer the joke, the better!
Use Teddy's totally covert code and see if the
joke's on you! For code, go to page 58.

WA HA HA HA HA HA HA HA HA

Q: _ _ _ _   _ _ _   _ _ _
   D S Z G S Z H G D L

_ _ _ _ _   _ _ _
S Z M W H Y F G

_ _ _ _ ,   _ _ _ _ ?
X Z M G X O Z K

A: _   _ _ _ _ _ !
   Z X O L X P

WA HA HA HA
HA HA HA
HO HA
HA HO

DREAM SCHEME

What if you were Miss or Mister Lucky? What if you won the lottery or became a movie star and everyone wanted your autograph? Rank your top 5 all-time dreams!

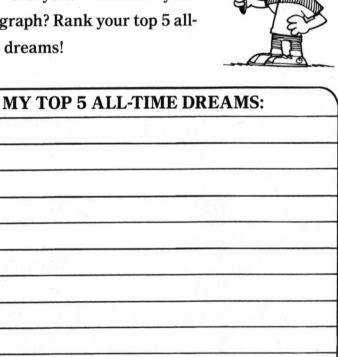

MY TOP 5 ALL-TIME DREAMS:

1.

2.

3.

4.

5.

MISS OR MISTER LUCKY!

WHAT IS YOUR FAN SAYING?

WHAT IS YOUR MOVIE DIRECTOR SAYING?

DRAW YOUR PICTURE HERE

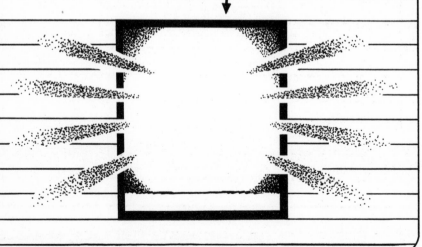

CELEBRITY CRAZE

Check out pages 61–62 for a thrilling grammar
lesson from Ms. Clarke!

MAKE A LIST OF THE MOST
FABULOUS WORDS YOU CAN THINK OF:

1. Noun:

2. Noun (plural):

3. Noun (plural):

4. Noun:

5. Verb:

6. Adverb:

7. Verb:

8. Adverb:

9. Verb:

10. Noun:

11. Noun:

12. Noun:

13. Noun:

14. Noun:

15. Noun:

YOU'RE A CELEBRITY!

NOW USE YOUR LIST
TO FILL IN THE BLANKS!

I am the Greatest!

One day I'll become a famous _____ .
1.

I'll wear lots of _____ and _____ , and
2. 3.

travel to _____ every week. My fans will
4.

_____ _____ and shout to me!
5. 6.

When I _____ _____ , everyone
7. 8.

will _____ as I dazzle the crowd. After
9.

my _____ , I will race away in my
10.

_____ . Finally, I can take a _____
11. 12.

in a twenty-five-acre _____ that over-
13.

looks the breathtaking _____ , the place
14.

I call _____ .
15.

NOW **THAT'S** GREATNESS!

GUESS WHAT?

How big is your brain? Using Francis's alphabet (page 39), decode these weird and wacky facts.

$\overline{13}$ $\overline{2}$ $\overline{9}$ $\overline{6}$ $\overline{1}$ $\overline{11}$ $\overline{21}$ $\overline{20}$ $\overline{21}$

$\overline{13}$ $\overline{10}$ $\overline{24}$ $\overline{6}$ $\overline{14}$ $\overline{13}$ $\overline{23}$ $\overline{20}$ $\overline{13}$

$\overline{11}$ $\overline{21}$ $\overline{26}$ $\overline{8}$ $\overline{24}$ $\overline{22}$ $\overline{13}$ $\overline{23}$ $\overline{23}$ $\overline{11}$ $\overline{22}$ $\overline{8}$ $\overline{25}$

$\overline{16}$ $\overline{11}$ $\overline{10}$ $\overline{14}$ $\overline{3}$ $\overline{11}$ $\overline{23}$ $\overline{16}$ $\overline{7}$ $\overline{13}$ $\overline{23}$ $\overline{23}$ $\overline{24}$.

$\overline{18}\ \overline{11}\ \overline{21}\ \overline{12}\ \overline{8}\ \overline{9}\ \overline{24}\quad \overline{20}\ \overline{21}$

$\overline{6}\ \overline{1}\ \overline{13}\ \overline{20}\ \overline{23}\ \overline{13}\ \overline{21}\ \overline{25}\quad \overline{13}\ \overline{14}\ \overline{8}$

$\overline{6}\ \overline{14}\ \overline{13}\ \overline{20}\ \overline{21}\ \overline{8}\ \overline{25}$

$\overline{6}\ \overline{11}\quad \overline{2}\ \overline{20}\ \overline{26}\ \overline{12}$

$\overline{26}\ \overline{11}\ \overline{26}\ \overline{11}\ \overline{21}\ \overline{10}\ \overline{6}\ \overline{24}$.

MRS. GODFREY'S ESSAY QUESTIONS ARE SO INVIGORATING!

$\overline{20}\ \overline{21}\qquad \overline{2}\ \overline{8}\ \overline{14}\ \overline{10}\qquad \overline{2}\ \overline{8}\ \overline{11}\ \overline{2}\ \overline{23}\ \overline{8}$

$\overline{13}\ \overline{6}\ \overline{8}\qquad \overline{26}\ \overline{1}\ \overline{20}\ \overline{23}\ \overline{20}\qquad \overline{2}\ \overline{8}\ \overline{2}\ \overline{2}\ \overline{8}\ \overline{14}\ \overline{24}$

$\overline{13}\ \overline{24}\qquad \overline{23}\ \overline{11}\ \overline{21}\ \overline{3}\qquad \overline{13}\ \overline{24}\qquad \overline{24}\ \overline{20}\ \overline{17}$

$\overline{6}\ \overline{1}\ \overline{11}\ \overline{10}\ \overline{24}\ \overline{13}\ \overline{21}\ \overline{25}$

$\overline{9}\ \overline{8}\ \overline{13}\ \overline{14}\ \overline{24}\qquad \overline{13}\ \overline{3}\ \overline{11}$.

TRUE LIFE COMIX

Have you ever imagined your life in cartoons? Nate has! Help create Nate's true-life story by filling in the speech bubbles.

ULTRA-NATE'S COMIX HEROES

Nate wants to become a famous cartoonist some-day! He even created his own comic, "The Wacky Adventures of Doctor Cesspool." Can you find all 20 of the cartooning heroes below in the super search on the next page?

ARCHIE

BATMAN

CATWOMAN

CHARLIE BROWN

FANTASTIC FOUR

GARFIELD

INCREDIBLE HULK

IRON MAN

LEX LUTHOR

LINUS

LUCY

MARMADUKE

POPEYE

SNOOPY

SPIDER-MAN

SUPERMAN

THE JOKER

WOLVERINE

WONDER WOMAN

X-MEN

```
E O A E M R A R E W Y B C T F
W T E T Y P O O N S E A H F K
O D A H N E K U D A M R A M X
L L E E S U P E R M A N R R L
V E N J F I E O Y W T E L L O
E I R O N M A N P A H N I N R
R F K K A E M N S R K A E B M
I R L E X L U T H O R M B A E
N A M R E D I P S C X O R T B
E G T I R C E I H M R W O M N
X A U E F E L I N M O T W A S
I L W O N D E R W O M A N N U
K L U H E L B I D E R C N I N
A R E C E U I H C D W N L N I
X A I A Y A A O E P M H L A L
```

"Doctor Cesspool"
by Nate

BETTER THAN BEST BONE-CRUSHING TEAM NAMES

Nate's super psyched! Coach names him captain of his fleeceball team. Now Nate needs an awesome team name. Can you help him?

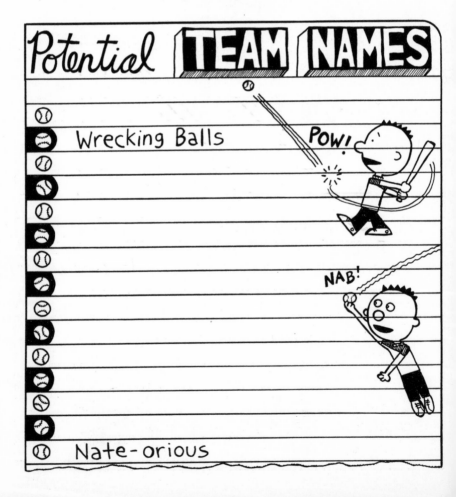

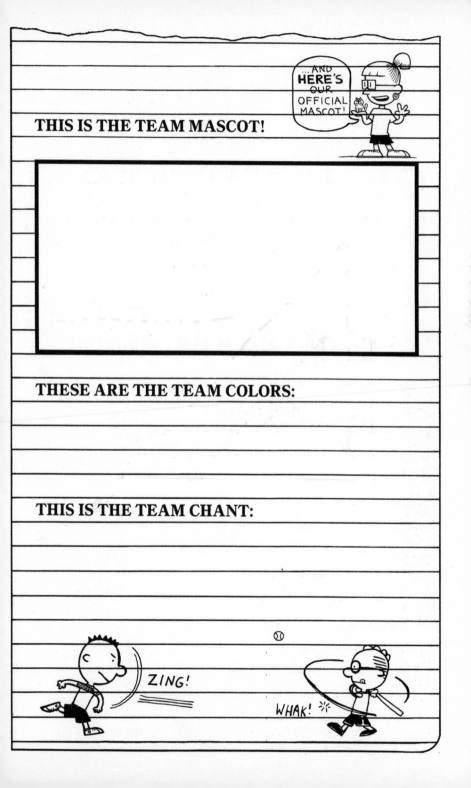

Watch out! Gina, the know-it-all, has her own ideas. Help Gina come up with names like these:

GINA's TEAM NAMES

- Warm & Fuzzies
- Kuddle Kittens
- United We Stand

THIS IS **KUDDLES**! MY OLDEST AND MOST FAVOR-ITE STUFFED ANIMAL!

SHE'S **PUFFY**, JUST LIKE A FLEECEBALL! **SEE**?

DOODLE MANIA!

Does your notebook look like Nate's? Do you scribble your crush's name or design your dream car? Dare to DOODLE!

THE FORTU-NA-TOR

Can Nate make his fortune come true?

SAVED BY THE BELL

Did you hear the bell? School's out! Nate has lots of cool after-school fun—soccer, scout meetings, creating comix, and drumming in his band! How about you?

TOP 5 THINGS FOR AFTER-SCHOOL FUN:

1.

2.

3.

4.

5.

Find all 20 after-school activities in this super word scramble and move to the head of the class!

ACTING

BALLET

BAND

BASEBALL

BASKETBALL

CHEERLEADING

CHOIR

FRISBEE

HOCKEY

ICE-SKATING

KARATE

KICKBALL

PAINTING

PIANO

PING-PONG

POTTERY

READING

SCHOOL PAPER

TAP DANCING

VIDEO GAMES

N G Y A T E I R H G S I C L O
O N R L J T I O N E C G N L T
U I E Q K O C I P E D F W A L
P D T I H K T H S N F N P B E
X A T C E N X K A Q R D V K E
L E O Y I P A B Q E A O I C B
L L P A E T I M P N K M D I S
A R P T I V M A C M R P E K I
B E U N A T P I N U J J O R R
E E G U E L N H P O V K G E F
S H S L O G S G N I T C A A N
A C L O G N O P G N I P M D I
B A H A E T A R A K W W E I A
B C L L A B T E K S A B S N B
S T R N B O B A Q M L Z A G C

RRRRINNNGG!!

NATE! TODAY AFTER SCHOOL WILL BE **FUN**, YES?

HM?

TRASH

DETENTION CONVENTION

Where there's Nate, there's trouble. His middle name is mischief. Just kidding! (Nate does not have a middle name.)

Nate is no stranger to the detention room. Do you ever get in trouble?

Or do you get gold stars like Gina, the honor roll student?

TOP 5 TIMES YOU'VE BEEN IN TROUBLE:
(UH-OH!)

1.

2.

3.

4.

5.

TOP 5 GOLD STAR MOMENTS:

1.

2.

3.

4.

5.

EXCLAMATION GAME

Things don't always go your way just because you're awesome. You decide what Nate's saying or thinking—fill in the bubbles!

UGH!

WHOA! WHAT IS NATE SAYING?

HONOR ROLL, OR NOT?

Gina may be a triple-A student.

But DETENTION is awaiting her!

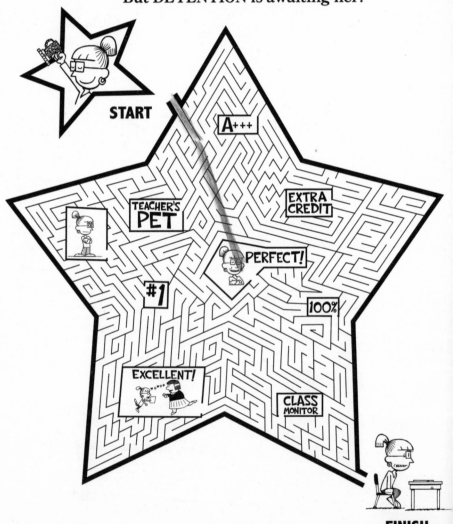

SUPER SCRIBBLE GAME

This scribble is going to turn into . . . what?

Don't forget to write a caption for it!

NO-SNACK ZONE

Does your school cafeteria stink like egg salad?
Eww, gross!

HERE ARE SOME OF THE FOODS NATE HATES!

Prunes

Egg salad

Squishy bananas

LIST YOUR TOP 10 WORST FOODS EVER!

1.

2.

3.

4.

5.

6.

7.

8.

9.

10.

YOUR TRUE-LIFE STORY

You are a cartoonist. Here's your chance to draw YOUR true-life story.

I PLAY _____.   I HAVE A PET _____.

(sport or instrument)	**(real or imaginary)**
MY BEST FRIEND	**MY FAVORITE FOOD**

I LIVE IN _____. I ALWAYS WEAR _____.

MY FAVORITE BOOK   **MY FAVORITE MOVIE**

HOW'S THE GRAPHIC NOVEL COMING ALONG?

GOOD. I'M WRITING ABOUT WHAT HAPPENED IN THE THIRD INNING.

WAIT A MINUTE! YOU **STRUCK OUT** IN THE THIRD INNING!

YEAH. SO?

ACCORDING TO **THIS**, YOU HIT A 3-RUN **HOMER!**

I'M JUST MAKING THE STORYLINE MORE INTERESTING.

...AND THEN YOU SAVED A KID IN THE BLEACHERS FROM **CHOKING** ON A **HOT DOG**??

IT'S CALLED "ARTISTIC LICENSE."

TRIVIA TEST!

How well do you know Big Nate?

It's time to test your Nate Knowledge!

1. What is the name of Nate's math teacher?

    a. Mr. Galvin

    b. Mrs. Czerwicki

    c. Mr. Staples

    d. Mrs. Godfrey

YOU'LL USE MATH **EVERY** DAY FOR THE ~~REST OF~~ YOUR **LIFE!**

2. Who is Nate's ultimate enemy?

    a. Artur

    b. Randy

    c. Ellen

    d. Gina

3. What is Nate's most favorite food?

   a. Macaroni and cheese

   b. Cheez Doodles

   c. Spaghetti with meatballs

   d. Ice cream

4. What is the name of the animal that belongs to Mr. Eustis, Nate's neighbor?

   a. Pickles

   b. Kuddles

   c. Spitsy

   d. Spoffy

5. Nate's dad once wore this:

   a. A poncho

   b. Figure skates

   c. Glasses

   d. Batman Halloween costume

COMIX U CREATE

Tap into your inner artist!
You're the cartooning genius. Draw a comic
using Nate, Randy, and pie NOW!

?

YOUR TITLE HERE

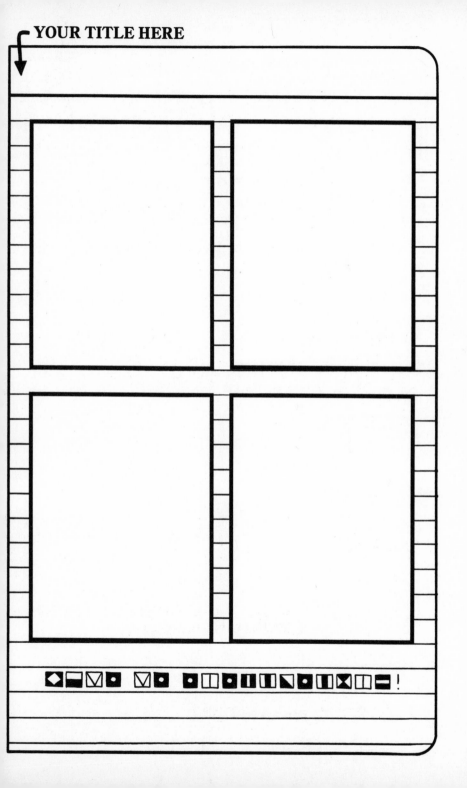

NATE WRIGHT PRESENTS

Nate loves to draw comix. Help him collect all his characters! Fill in the blanks so each Nate comix creation appears only once in every row, column, and box.

 D = **DOCTOR CESSPOOL**

 N = **NATE**

 E = **ELLEN**

 G = **GINA**

 F = **FRANCIS**

 T = **TEDDY**

 B = **BEN FRANKLIN**

 U = **ULTRA NATE**

 R = **RANDY BETANCOURT**

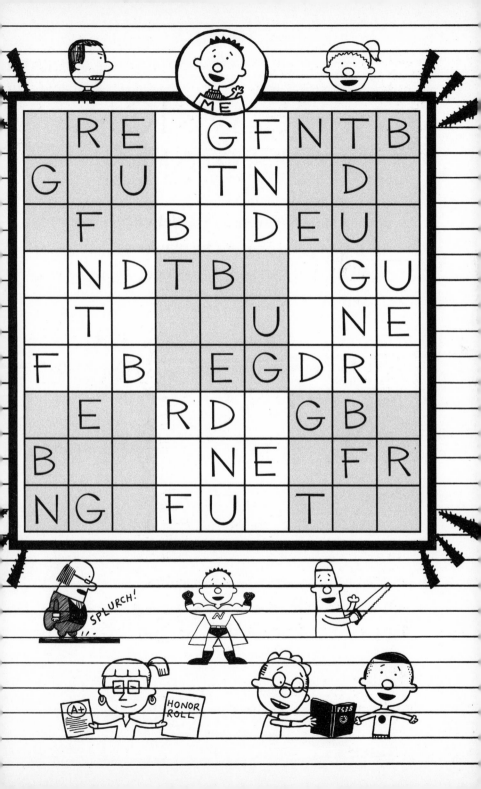

THE JOKE'S ON YOU!

Wanna laugh like crazy? Teddy's code (page 58) is the key to unlocking the hilarity!

Q: $\overline{D}\ \overline{S}\ \overline{Z}\ \overline{G}\quad \overline{W}\ \overline{L}$

$\overline{N}\ \overline{L}\ \overline{M}\ \overline{H}\ \overline{G}\ \overline{V}\ \overline{I}\ \overline{H}\quad \overline{I}\ \overline{V}\ \overline{Z}\ \overline{W}$

$\overline{V}\ \overline{E}\ \overline{V}\ \overline{I}\ \overline{B}\quad \overline{W}\ \overline{Z}\ \overline{B}$?

A: $\overline{G}\ \overline{S}\ \overline{V}\ \overline{R}\ \overline{I}$

$\overline{S}\ \overline{L}\ \overline{I}\ \overline{I}\ \overline{L}\ \overline{I}\ \overline{H}\ \overline{X}\ \overline{L}\ \overline{K}\ \overline{V}$!

HEH HEH!

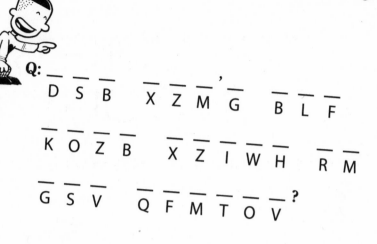

Q: _ _ _ _ _ _ _ , _ _ _ _
D S B   X Z M G   B L F

_ _ _ _ _ _ _ _ _ _ _ _
K O Z B   X Z I W H   R M

_ _ _ _ _ _ _ _ _ ?
G S V   Q F M T O V

A: _ _ _ _ _ _ _ _ _ _ _
Y V X Z F H V   G S V I V

_ _ _ _ _ _ _ _ _ _
Z I V   G L L   N Z M B

_ _ _ _ _ _ _ !
X S V V G Z H

HONK!
HONK
HONK!

DESTINED FOR GREATNESS

Help Nate with his list!

NATE COULD ACHIEVE GREATNESS IN...

1. Soccer
2. Music
3. Cartooning
4. Table football
5.
6.
7.
8.
9.
10.

HOW WILL YOU...

...SURPASS ALL OTHERS?

1. I'm in a rock band.
2. I will become a pilot.
3. I will swim with dolphins.
4.
5.
6.
7.
8.
9.
10.
11.
12.
13.
14.
15.

BATTER UP!

Take your team to victory! Draw lines from List A to List B to create the ultimate team names.

List A

Screaming

Fighting

Big Bad

Wicked

Awesome

Fierce & Fearless

Howling

Dazzling

Blazing

Death-Defying

List B

Starz

Superheroes

Hot Shots

Wildcats

Warriors

Pirates

Maniacs

Demons

Rebels

Cowboys

WRITE YOUR ULTIMATE
TEAM NAMES HERE:

_____

_____

_____

_____

_____

_____

_____

_____

_____

_____

WHERE'S PICASSO?

Are you destined to be a talented artist like Picasso? Pick up that pencil! Draw your self-portrait.

 # BIG BEN

Nate's a serious Ben Franklin fan, because Ben was an inventor AND a cartoonist, just like Nate! See how inventive you can be. Using the letters in Ben's name, try coming up with 25 other words!

BEN FRANKLIN

1.	16.
2.	17.
3.	18.
4.	19.
5.	20.
6.	21.
7.	22.
8.	23.
9.	24.
10.	25.
11.	
12.	
13.	
14.	
15.	

CELEBRITY FOR A DAY

Nate knows he's going to hit it big some day! What if YOU became a star and everyone knew YOUR name? Do you aim for fame?

CIRCLE YOUR TOP 5
CELEBRITY PROFESSIONS

Hollywood actor/actress

Genius scientist

Pro athlete

Broadway dancer

Doctor

President

Musician/rock star

Famous artist

Astronaut

Author

Animal trainer

Deep sea diver

Inventor

Race car driver

Video game creator

EL CAPITÁN

NATE'S BABY BOOK

Check out Nate's baby picture! He wasn't the cutest baby on the planet—look at that spiky hair!

WHAT ARE YOUR BABY FACTS?
(How would you know? You were only a baby!
Ask your parents!)

PLACE YOU WERE BORN:

_____

EYE COLOR:
Hazel

YOUR FIRST WORD:

_____

AGE WHEN YOU FIRST CRAWLED:

___6 months___

FAVORITE FOOD:

___macon'i___

FAVORITE TOY:

_____

FUNNIEST HABIT:
(Did you suck your thumb?
Or talk in gibberish?)

_____

Me and Ellen

PERFECT PARTNERS

Who will be Nate's partner for the school project?

PET PARADISE

Meet Spitsy, the dog who lives next door to Nate! He's a little bit crazy. He wears a collar that makes him look like a walking satellite dish and he is scared of the mailman. See if you can find all 20 kinds of pets below in the animal scramble on the next page!

PARAKEET

FERRET

TURTLE

GOLDFISH

PARROT

HORSE

MOUSE

LIZARD

CANARY

IGUANA

RABBIT

KITTEN

GUINEA PIG

SALAMANDER

SNAKE

HAMSTER

DOG

PIG

GERBIL

PONY

WURF!

G N O T G B K C T S W S L W H
Y Y T K H J H T A U N O T L S
F E R R E T Y L E A R U U R I
P Q J G M L A C K E B T E E F
A C Z O D M Y E U Y K T L L D
R G I P A E N I U G S A I E L
R C T N T T J M D M G Z R X O
O S D E I H M H A S A Z O A G
T E A U B O O H Y R A N A C P
R N Y N B T U R D G E R B I L
K Z T D A F S D S T X F G V X
Y G K M R U E Q T E F T V O I
X I K D I Z G I A U D L D F D
Q S H E T W K I U A H B R Z T
Y N O P W X M X S V U A O X X

Z...

DID YOU KNOW?

Decode these facts using Francis's code.
See page 39 for code.

$\overline{6}$ $\overline{1}$ $\overline{8}$ $\overline{18}$ $\overline{20}$ $\overline{25}$ $\overline{11}$ $\overline{26}$ $\overline{8}$ $\overline{13}$ $\overline{21}$

$\overline{14}$ $\overline{20}$ $\overline{25}$ $\overline{3}$ $\overline{8}$ $\overline{20}$ $\overline{24}$ $\overline{6}$ $\overline{1}$ $\overline{8}$

$\overline{23}$ $\overline{13}$ $\overline{14}$ $\overline{3}$ $\overline{8}$ $\overline{24}$ $\overline{6}$

$\overline{18}$ $\overline{11}$ $\overline{10}$ $\overline{21}$ $\overline{6}$ $\overline{13}$ $\overline{20}$ $\overline{21}$ $\overline{14}$ $\overline{13}$ $\overline{21}$ $\overline{3}$ $\overline{8}$

$\overline{20}$ $\overline{21}$ $\overline{6}$ $\overline{1}$ $\overline{8}$ $\overline{22}$ $\overline{11}$ $\overline{14}$ $\overline{23}$ $\overline{25}$

$\overline{13}$ $\overline{21}$ $\overline{25}$ $\overline{20}$ $\overline{6}$ $\overline{20}$ $\overline{24}$

$\overline{10}$ $\overline{21}$ $\overline{25}$ $\overline{8}$ $\overline{14}$ $\overline{22}$ $\overline{13}$ $\overline{6}$ $\overline{8}$ $\overline{14}$.

$\overline{6}$ $\overline{1}$ $\overline{8}$ $\overline{14}$ $\overline{8}$ $\quad$ $\overline{13}$ $\overline{14}$ $\overline{8}$ $\quad$ $\overline{13}$ $\overline{7}$ $\overline{11}$ $\overline{10}$ $\overline{6}$

$\overline{11}$ $\overline{21}$ $\overline{8}$ $\quad$ $\overline{1}$ $\overline{10}$ $\overline{21}$ $\overline{25}$ $\overline{14}$ $\overline{8}$ $\overline{25}$

$\overline{6}$ $\overline{14}$ $\overline{20}$ $\overline{23}$ $\overline{23}$ $\overline{20}$ $\overline{11}$ $\overline{21}$

$\overline{26}$ $\overline{8}$ $\overline{23}$ $\overline{23}$ $\overline{24}$ $\quad$ $\overline{20}$ $\overline{21}$ $\quad$ $\overline{6}$ $\overline{1}$ $\overline{8}$

$\overline{1}$ $\overline{10}$ $\overline{18}$ $\overline{13}$ $\overline{21}$ $\quad$ $\overline{7}$ $\overline{11}$ $\overline{25}$ $\overline{9}$.

REALLY? WHAT A **BRILLIANT** OBSERVATION, FRANCIS! I DIDN'T **KNOW** THAT!

CAN I SEE?

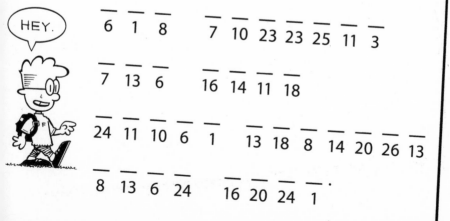

HEY.

$\overline{6}$ $\overline{1}$ $\overline{8}$ $\quad$ $\overline{7}$ $\overline{10}$ $\overline{23}$ $\overline{23}$ $\overline{25}$ $\overline{11}$ $\overline{3}$

$\overline{7}$ $\overline{13}$ $\overline{6}$ $\quad$ $\overline{16}$ $\overline{14}$ $\overline{11}$ $\overline{18}$

$\overline{24}$ $\overline{11}$ $\overline{10}$ $\overline{6}$ $\overline{1}$ $\quad$ $\overline{13}$ $\overline{18}$ $\overline{8}$ $\overline{14}$ $\overline{20}$ $\overline{26}$ $\overline{13}$

$\overline{8}$ $\overline{13}$ $\overline{6}$ $\overline{24}$ $\quad$ $\overline{16}$ $\overline{20}$ $\overline{24}$ $\overline{1}$.

HELP!
WHAT ARE THEY
SAYING?

You decide. Fill in the speech bubbles.

RAPPIN' AND RHYMIN'

Write a sentence that rhymes
with each underlined word.
You are a rapper!

YOU'VE HAD YOUR <u>FUN</u>,

_____ ,

YOU HEAR THEM <u>SAY</u>,

_____ .

NOW WE <u>FLY</u>,

_____ ,

AND THEN WE <u>MEET</u>,

_____ .

THE TIME IS <u>RIGHT</u>,

_____ ,

OH YES YOU <u>SEE</u>,

_____ .

WHO'S IN LOVE?

Nate likes Jenny. Jenny likes Artur. Nate hates Gina, but as Teddy says, "It's a fine line between hate and love." Nate needs help! Fill in the blanks so each person appears only once in every row, column, and box.

G = **GINA**

N = **NATE**

J = **JENNY**

A = **ARTUR**

HOW TO DRAW ME

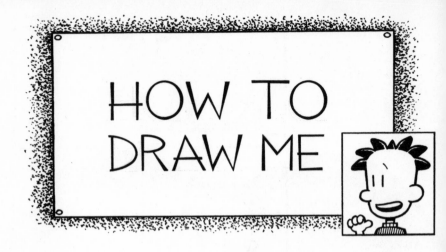

Follow Nate's step-by-step instructions
and bring him to life!

HINT: SKETCH LIGHTLY AT FIRST, THEN MAKE
LINES **BOLDER** TO FINISH YOUR DRAWING!

START WITH AN
OVAL. SEE HOW
IT'S WIDER AT
THE TOP?

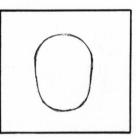

MAKE A SMALLER
OVAL. THERE'S
MY NOSE!

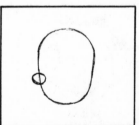

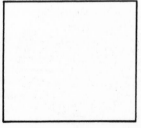

A LOOP (LIKE A BACKWARD "C") IS MY EAR.

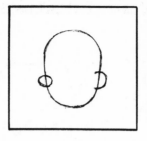

I HAVE SEVEN TUFTS OF HAIR. FOLLOW THE ARROWS!

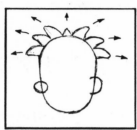

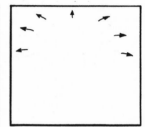

MY EYES ARE EASY TO DRAW. THEY'RE TWO STRAIGHT LINES!

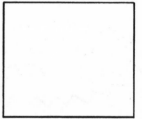

NOW ADD MY MOUTH SO I CAN SAY SOMETHING!

COLOR IN MY **HAIR**, ADD A NECK AND SHOULDERS, AND YOU'RE **DONE!**

MOST EMBARRASSING MOMENTS EVER

Do you ever wish you could run and hide? Nate's no stranger to awkward moments—he's the king of embarrassing situations. The worst was when he accidentally spilled egg salad on his crush Jenny's head!

RANK THESE FROM 1 TO 10. 10 IS THE MOST EMBARRASSING!

5 Being caught picking your nose

5 Having to wear the ugly snowman sweater from Aunt Gladys to school

5 Slipping in the hall after the janitor waxed the floors

10 Throwing up on the roller coaster

10 When you show up wearing the same shirt as your lab partner

10 When your mom kisses you big time while dropping you off at school

_5_ Looking cross-eyed in your school pictures

_5_ The cat pees on your feet

_6_ When you're picked second-to-last in gym class

_10_ You're all ready to perform for the talent show and your voice gets all scratchy

_4_ Your hair is sticking straight up all day and you have no idea

_10_ Laughing so hard that snot comes out of your nose

_10_ You spill orange juice on your shirt at lunch and it looks like puke

_4_ You have to dance with your teachers at your school dance

MUSICAL MADNESS

WHO'S READY TO ROCK?!

Nate is the rockin' drummer in his band, Enslave the Mollusk! Now it's your turn. Take the stage and find all the instruments in this hidden word puzzle!

FLUTE

TROMBONE

TRUMPET

GUITAR

CYMBALS

TRIANGLE

SAXOPHONE

PIANO

VIOLIN

TUBA

BASS

VIOLA

DRUMS

FRENCH HORN

HARP

CLARINET

PICCOLO

TAMBOURINE

M	E	N	P	U	A	T	P	L	O	R	A
I	L	U	R	S	O	N	T	S	A	T	R
O	T	R	U	M	P	E	T	T	N	U	R
U	G	E	L	G	N	A	I	R	T	B	E
O	V	E	N	I	R	U	O	B	M	A	T
L	T	X	R	O	G	H	N	A	O	C	U
O	H	A	R	P	H	I	B	S	N	Y	L
C	L	O	L	C	L	P	A	S	U	M	F
C	V	E	N	O	B	M	O	R	T	B	Y
I	Y	E	I	A	I	E	L	X	A	A	C
P	R	V	A	M	I	V	G	E	A	L	T
F	D	R	U	M	S	P	T	S	S	S	B

WILD WORLD RECORDS

Nate knows he's got the right stuff to stand out. He's ready to surpass all others and set a world record! For longest fingernails? No! Speed eating? Maybe! He does LOVE Cheez Doodles!

CHECK OUT THESE SUPER WEIRD WORLD RECORDS:

Longest eyebrows

Largest feet

Longest nose

Tallest man

Highest hair

Biggest cookie

Fastest talker

Most T-shirts worn at once

Most worms swallowed

Most tennis balls held in one hand

Most consecutive pogo stick jumps

Longest nonstop TV watching

WHAT WOULD <u>YOU</u> SET A RECORD IN?

1.

2.

3.

4.

5. Biggest smile

6.

7.

8.

9. Loudest burp

10.

11.

12.

13. Most chocolate eaten

14.

15.

SUPER SCRIBBLE GAME

How fast can you play the scribble game?

Don't forget to write a caption for it:

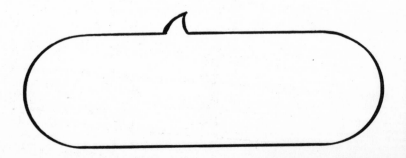

SCHOOL RULES

Nate cruises the school halls with confidence. But where does he always end up? DETENTION!

WHAT ARE YOUR ALL-TIME FAVORITE SCHOOL SUBJECTS?

1.

2.

3.

4.

5.

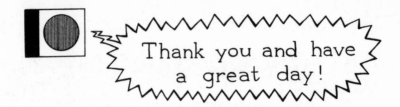

Thank you and have a great day!

Did you hear the bell? School's in session. See if you can solve the puzzle and figure out all of Nate's daily subjects.

CLUES

ACROSS

3. Where you might make a birdhouse or a pencil box.

4. Paying attention in this subject will help you solve this puzzle!

8. Here "hola" means "hello."

10. Nate's favorite class.

11. You might practice these lines: "Romeo, O Romeo, wherefore art thou Romeo?"

14. In this class, you might be allowed to go on www.bignatebooks.com!

DOWN

1. How many continents are there?

2. After lunch, you have _____ .

5. Where you create a poetry portfolio.

6. Let's pick teams.

7. Name the basic food groups.

9. Today we're going to dissect a frog.

12. If x is 2 and y is 3, x + y = ?

13. Tater tots and mystery meat.

15. Who wants to play the triangle?

WHOA!
WHAT'S HAPPENING?

Fill in the speech bubbles

and create your own crazy comix!

ROCK AND ROLLIN'

It's time to rock out, Nate style! Fill in words
below to create your own band names.

1. FUNKY _____ _____

2. _____ _____ TIME

3. _____ DIAMOND _____

4. WILD _____ _____

5. _____ BLUE _____

6. _____ _____ FORTUNE

7. LAUGHING _____ _____

8. _____ SECRET _____

9. _____ _____ MACHINE

10. GALAXY _____

FABULOUS FUN-O-METER

Use Nate's Fun-o-Meter and rank each activity!

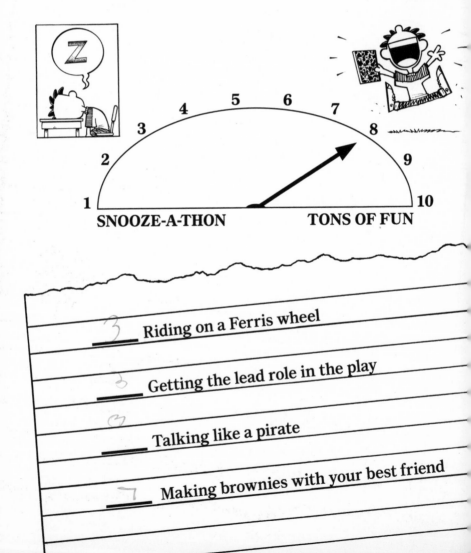

SNOOZE-A-THON   **TONS OF FUN**

_3_ Riding on a Ferris wheel

_3_ Getting the lead role in the play

_3_ Talking like a pirate

_7_ Making brownies with your best friend

_____ Building a sandcastle

_____ Watching the sun set

_____ Trick-or-treating at Halloween

_____ Riding the school bus

_____ Eating cotton candy

_____ Going to the dentist

_____ Cruisin' the hood on my skateboard

_____ Playing table football

_____ Watching your favorite team

_____ Building a fort

_____ Drawing comix

_____ Playing dodgeball in gym class

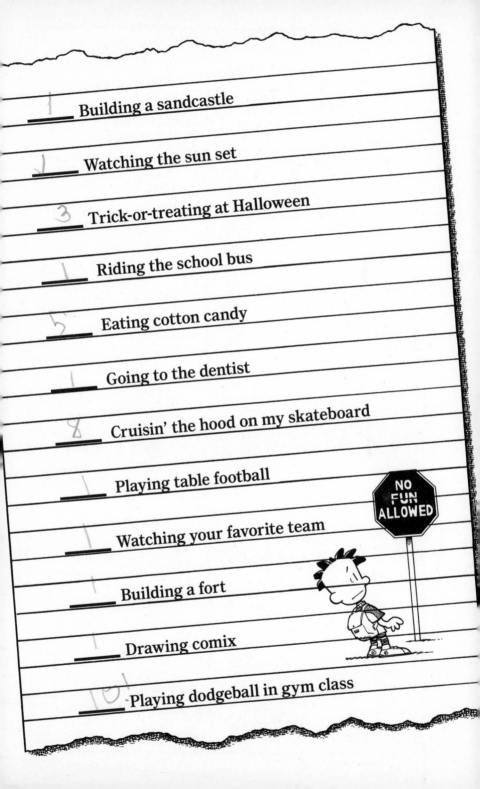

NO FUN ALLOWED

DOCTOR CESSPOOL TO THE RESCUE?

Help Nate finish his cartoon about this wacky doctor—looks like trouble!

EXTRA CREDIT

☐ YES ☐ NO

SUPER SPOFF

What's a SPOFF? The coolest thing ever!

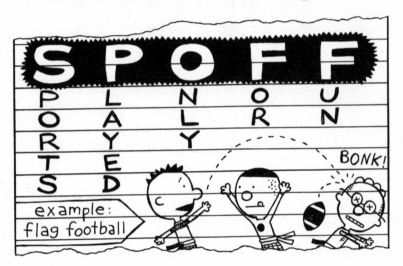

Nate's dying to win the SPOFF championship and take home the ultimate prize—the Spoffy! Help him find all the hidden words so he can surpass all others!

G O G L S Z L U E C A O F L
R E M A L L L H R Y L L D T
D E H R T A A F U E O P K L
E R O H D E B A R O L E S A
G A L F E H T E R U T P A C
M U R R H N O H G P U H F T
O Q U E B T O C E D B A A E
O S E E A C F T O R O B A M
A R H Z K T G O N R B D E D
H U A E A G A C E I E A U D
G O Y T G E L S R S M Y L T
E F N A C E F P R E F D R L
D U E G R E V O R D E R A H
Z F G E V S H H S U D L S B

FLOOR HOCKEY

CAPTURE THE FLAG

FLAG FOOTBALL

BADMINTON

DODGEBALL

FOURSQUARE

TETHERBALL

SPUD

RED ROVER

HOPSCOTCH

FREEZE TAG

HORSE

WHACK!

WHO DO YOU THINK YOU ARE?

SPOTLIGHT ON...

YOU

Nickname:

WHAT'S YOUR SIGN?

Birthday:

Astrological sign:

Song you play over and over:

Most amazing book you've ever read:

Coolest place you've traveled to:

Best friend:

Pet:

Celebrity crush:

Greatest movie you've ever seen:

Dream job:

Biggest talent:

Favorite time of year:

Your signature dance move:

#1 for weekend fun:

Best place on Earth:

Proudest moment:

Your hero:

NO LESSON PLAN!

Not every teacher is boring. Help Nate find the fun teachers at P.S. 38. Fill in the blanks so each appears only once in every row, column, and box.

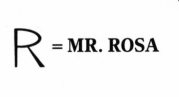 R = **MR. ROSA**

 S = **MRS. SHIPULSKI**

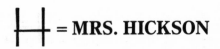 H = **MRS. HICKSON**

 C = **COACH CALHOUN**

S	C	H	R
H		C	S
R			
	S		

OUT-OF-CONTROL LOCKER

Nate's locker is overflowing with cool stuff—

No joke! What are your must-haves for your locker?

TOP 25 MUST-HAVES:

1.

2. Smelly socks

3.

4. Poster of _____

(Fill in your favorite celebrity!)

5.

6.

7.

8.

9.

10. Cheez Doodles

11.

12.

13.

14.

15. Gym clothes

16.

17.

18.

19.

20.

21.

22.

23.

24.

25.

KLIK!

LIFE IS CRAZY

Life can be kind of crazy sometimes . . . you never know what might happen! You decide the story behind each scene.

THIS DOESN'T LOOK GOOD!

YIKES!

WHAT'S GOING ON?

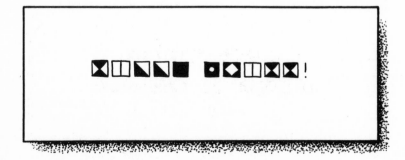

MAKING THE GRADE

Are you an A student all the way? What makes the grade for you? You're the teacher now!

**REVIEW THE LIST BELOW
AND GRADE EACH ACTIVITY:
A, B, C, D, OR . . . (UH-OH) F!**

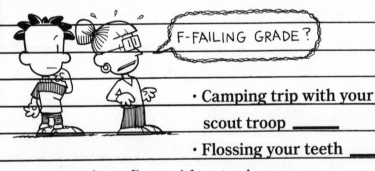

F-FAILING GRADE?

· Camping trip with your
  scout troop _____

· Flossing your teeth _____

· Root-beer float with extra ice cream _____

· Meeting Mickey Mouse _____

· Taking your dog for a walk _____

· Doing the hokey pokey _____

· Finishing your science homework _____

· Riding your bike _____

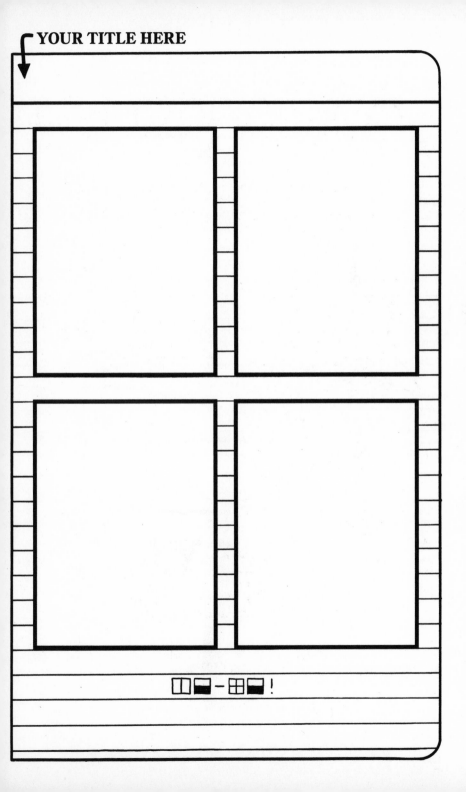

YOUR TITLE HERE

SUPER SCRIBBLE GAME

Can you play the scribble game in 10 seconds?

Don't forget to write a caption for it:

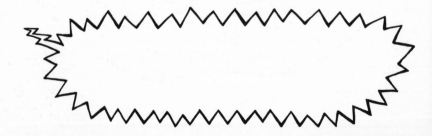

SHOWDOWN!

Mrs. Godfrey would rather be eating lemon squares.

CHEER CLUB

Nate's no cheerleader, but he sure looks cute in his uniform! Just kidding. Still, Nate has TONS of spirit—he's his own biggest fan! Help cheer Nate on to greatness!

FINISH THE CHEERS.
RHYME WITH THE UNDERLINED WORD!

Our team's on top, our team's on <u>top</u>,
Once we start we can't be _____.

We're number one, we're not number <u>two</u>,
We're gonna beat the socks off _____.

Our team won't take <u>defeat</u>,
Our team won't feel the _____,
Our team just can't be _____!

NOW MAKE UP YOU OWN CHEERS!

Hey, hey, get out of our <u>way</u>,
'Cause today is the day we will _____.

Everybody in the <u>stands</u>,
Clap your _____!

Come on team, let's have some <u>fun</u>,
Come on team, we're number _____!

We've got spirit, yes we <u>do</u>!
We've got spirit, how 'bout _____?

OUTBURSTS!

What's going on in each picture?
Fill in the speech bubbles!

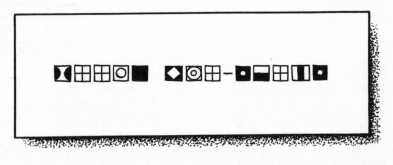

feeble pop-up →

BOOF!

WIDE WORLD OF NATE

Nate knows he's a big deal, and so is his name! Using the letters in his name see if you can make at least 20 other words!

BIG NATE

1.
2.
3.
4.
5.
6.
7.
8.
9.
10.
11.
12.
13.
14.
15.
16.
17.
18.
19.
20.

NATE IQ TEST

What makes Nate tick? How much do you know about Nate, the notorious mischief maker?

CIRCLE THE CORRECT ANSWER!

1. What's the name of Nate's comic strip?

   a. Max, the Mad Scientist

   b. Kooky Carl

   c. Daredevil Marvin

   d. Doctor Cesspool

   e. Magician Harry and Rex Rabbit

2. In which sport does Nate become a captain?

   a. Basketball

   b. Soccer

   c. Fleeceball

   d. Baseball

   e. Table football

THINK THINK THINK THINK THINK THINK THINK THINK

3. What is Nate's next-door neighbor's name?

a. Mrs. Shipulski

b. Mr. Galvin

c. Mr. Eustis

d. Mr. Nichols

e. Mrs. Czerwicki

4. Which is the one period where Nate hasn't gotten detention?

a. English

b. Art

c. Gym

d. Lunch

e. None of the above

** EXTRA CREDIT: Nate and Gina have to work together on a school project about...

a. Christopher Columbus

b. George Washington

c. Ben Franklin

d. Betsy Ross

e. Thomas Jefferson

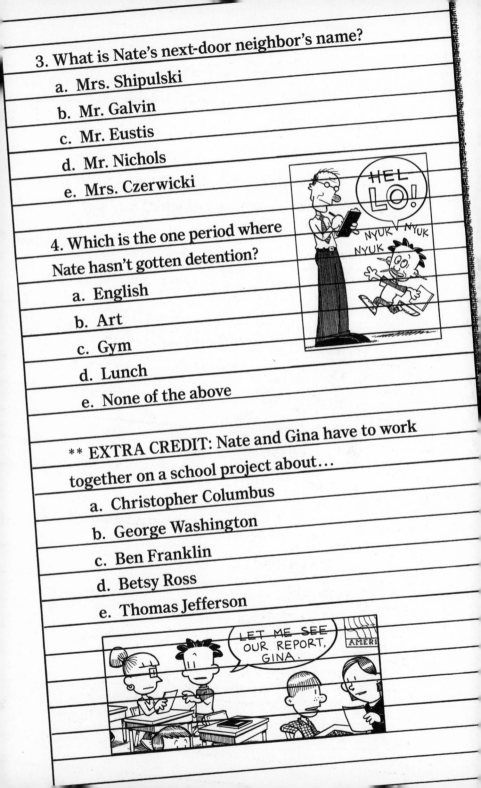

G S R H   L M V '   T V M R F H   ___!

MASTERMIND

Are you a whiz with words? Test your super skills!
Using the letters in "encyclopedia" below, see if you
can create 30 other words!

ENCYCLOPEDIA

1.
2.
3.
4.
5.
6.
7.
8.
9.
10.
11.
12.
13.
14.
15.
16.
17.
18.
19.
20.
21.
22.
23.
24.
25.
26.
27.
28.
29.
30.

LAUGH-A-MINUTE

What's so funny? Write speech bubbles and go for the BIGGEST laughs!

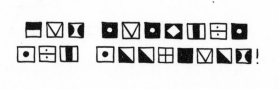

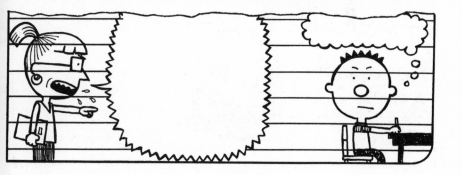

ONE OF A KIND

Nate's known for his super-spiky hair (check it out!) and his genius ideas . . . or at least he thinks so! What makes  you unique? How do you stand out from the crowd?

NAME THE THINGS THAT MAKE YOU ONE OF A KIND:

1.
2.
3. Killer laugh
4.
5. Sassy smirk
6.
7.
8.
9.
10.
11.

12. Sweet soccer skills

13.

14.

15.

16. Funny faces

17.

18.

19.

20.

21. Colorful socks

22.

23.

24.

25.

ATHLETE OF THE YEAR

Nate loves sports. Well . . . most sports. Fill in the blanks so each sport appears only once in every row, column, and box.

 V = VOLLEYBALL

 B = BASKETBALL

 T = TABLE FOOTBALL

 D = DODGEBALL

 R = RHYTHMIC GYMNASTICS

 Y = YOGA

 H = HOCKEY

 S = SOCCER

 F = FLEECE-BALL

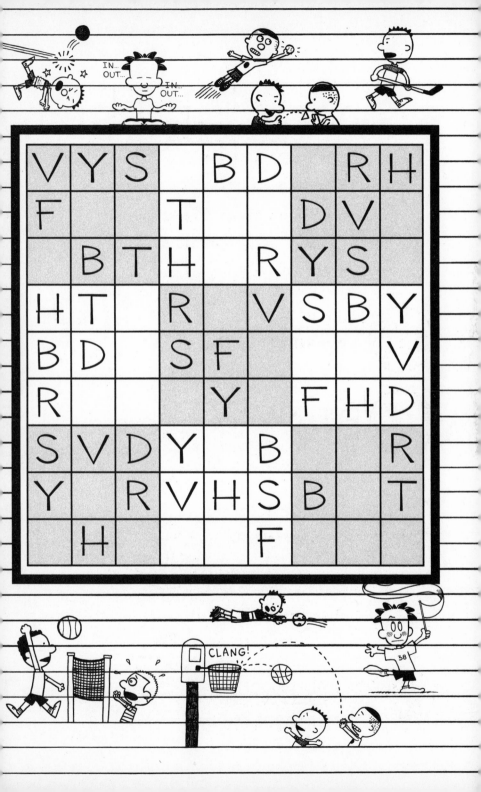

SAY CHEESE!

Smile BIG—it's time for your photo op! Create your own photo album by drawing in these major moments.

Me and Ellen

YOU AND YOUR BEST FRIEND ON THE FIRST DAY OF SCHOOL

YOUR BEST BIRTHDAY PARTY EVER

YOUR COOLEST HALLOWEEN COSTUME

SHOUT IT OUT!

What are these characters saying? Fill in the speech bubbles!

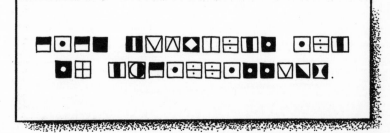

COMIX BY U!

You're the cartoonist now! Create a comic using
Mrs. Godfrey, Nate, and a detention slip!

YOUR TITLE HERE

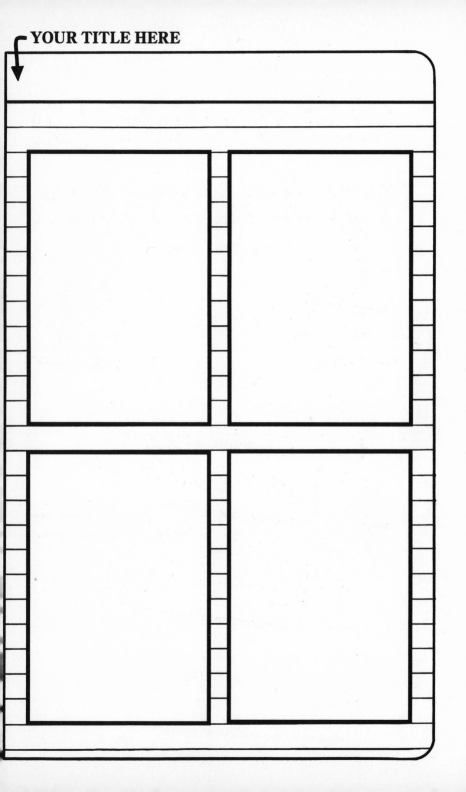

ANIMAL ANTICS

Are you partial to parakeets? A die-hard dog lover? Or crazy for cats, like Nate's big sister, Ellen? Whether or not you have a pet, it doesn't matter. Mix and match these words to make the PERFECT PET NAME!

Mister

Cuckoo

Cuddle

Dexter

Arlo

Dizzy

Super

Slick

Rex

Molly

Fluff

Cool

Fuzz

Whisker

Flopper

Scooter

Cocoa

Big

Toot

Pepper

King

Duke

Max

Man

Lady

Bug

Cruiser

Mo

Miss

Princess

WRITE YOUR PERFECT PET NAMES HERE:

_____

_____

_____

_____

_____

_____

_____

_____

_____

_____

_____

BEST DAYS EVER!

What makes you happier than ever? Describe your top 15 dream days!

BEST DAYS EVER

1.

2.

3. Winning the _____ tournament

(put in your favorite sport)

4.

5.

6.

7. Unlimited Halloween candy!

8.

9.

10. **When your crush talks to you for the first time EVER**

11.

12.

13.

14.

15.

ANSWER KEY

NATE'S TOP SECRET CODE (p. 5)
Busted!
Oh how I hate her!
Clueless as usual

INVENT-A-COMIX (p. 9)
Semaphore: Spike it, Ben!

CAST OF CHARACTERS (pp. 11–13)
My best friend
My worst enemy
Bossy older sister
My other best friend
Does not know how to work the DVD player
Annoying rival
My true love
Big bully
Drama queen
Ultimate dog nerd
Nate calls him Todd
Forces Nate to slow dance with her

POETRY SLAM: RHYME TIME
(pp. 24–25)
Semaphores:
You are a poet and you did not know it.
A Limerick to Mrs. Godfrey
She is called by the name of Godzilla,
And yes, she's one scary gorilla,
Watch out or she'll eat you,
Her pop quizzes will beat you,
If you act just like Gina, you'll thrill her.

NATE'S WACKY WORLD (p. 19)

```
A H I I M S P O F F O T K
N O T F R E K C O L O G R
I M H R R S I C N A R F Y
G E L D O O D Z E E H C E
N W N L S N A A A G A L Y
Z O F I A S J T C R L E D
N R O R P B N E T E T N N
R K R I N E E O N E O U A
A R T I S T O C I N D E R
E S U S T N Y K E B Y D O
Y O N O I T N E T E D W Y
F G E N O E G G S A L A D
N T G O A L I E F N R F D
```

POP QUIZ! (p. 29)

Math—

Gym—

Social
Studies—

Science—

English—

Art—

QUESTION OF THE DAY (p. 30)
None! That is what students are for!

COOL COMIX! (p. 33)
Semaphore: Now you are a cartooning genius,
just like Nate!

FRANCIS'S FANTASTIC SECRET ALPHABET (p. 39)
In *Big Nate on a Roll*, look out for Peter Pan, Timber Scouts,
and detention, of course.

BEST BUDS
(p. 35)

N	F	S	T
S	T	F	N
T	S	N	F
F	N	T	S

IN THE CAFETORIUM (p. 44)

		¹R					²T		³B		
⁴S	P	I	N	A	C	H		U	R		
		C					N		U		
		⁵E	G	G	S		A		S		
		C					F		S		
⁶P	E	A				⁷L	I	V	E	R	
		K		⁹B			S		L		
	⁸C	E	L	E	R	Y		S		
		E						S		
		T						P		¹¹B
								R		R
			¹⁰T	O	M	A	T	O		O
								U		C
			¹²F	I	¹³S	H	S	T	I	C	K
					N					O
¹⁴L	I	M	A	B	E	A	N			L
					I					I
					L				

THE CHAMP (p. 46)

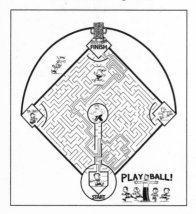

PLAY BALL!

TEDDY'S TOP SECRET CODE (p. 59)
All MLB umpires must wear black underwear while on the job!
The tallest player in the NBA is currently Yao Ming.
He is seven feet, six inches.

IT'S CRAZY IN 3010! (p. 64)
Semaphore: The future is calling you!

DAD IS NOT A BLAST (p. 51)
1. True
2. False
3. True
4. False

CHEEZ DOODLE ALERT (p. 55)

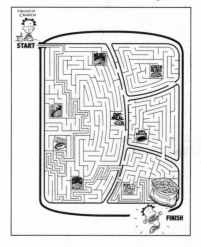

ANOTHER TEST! (pp. 56–57)

1.	False	7.	False
2.	True	8.	False
3.	False	9.	False
4.	False	10.	True
5.	True	11.	True
6.	True	12.	False

DRAW-A-THON (p. 67)
Semaphore: Table football is one of Nate's best sports.

TEACHER TROUBLE (p. 69)

S	G	C	P
C	P	G	S
P	C	S	G
G	S	P	C

COSMIC COOKIES (p. 70)
You have a secret admirer.
You will live in the lap of luxury.
You will travel to the moon.

WEIRD BUT TRUE (p. 73)
The titan beetle can grow up to eight inches in length.

TRASHED! (p. 81)

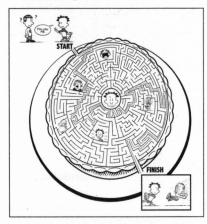

THE GANG'S ALL HERE! (p. 87)

S	D	G	A	N	T	F	J	E
F	T	J	E	S	G	N	A	D
N	A	E	F	J	D	S	T	G
A	J	F	T	G	E	D	N	S
T	E	S	N	D	J	A	G	F
D	G	N	S	A	F	T	E	J
E	S	T	G	F	A	J	D	N
G	N	D	J	T	S	E	F	A
J	F	A	D	E	N	G	S	T

COMIX BY U! (p. 89)
Semaphore: This smells like trouble!

TOP JOKESTER (pp. 90–91)
Q: How can you make an egg laugh?
A: Tell it a yolk!
Q: What has two hands but can't clap?
A: A clock!

GUESS WHAT? (pp. 96–97)
A python in Australia once swallowed four golf balls.
Monkeys in Thailand are trained to pick coconuts.
In Peru people ate chili peppers as long as six thousand years ago.

ULTRA-NATE'S COMIX HEROES (p. 101)

E	O	A	E	M	R	A	R	E	W	Y	B	C	T	F
W	T	E	T	Y	P	O	O	N	S	E	A	H	F	K
O	D	A	H	N	E	K	U	D	A	M	R	A	M	X
L	L	E	E	S	U	P	E	R	M	A	N	R	R	L
V	E	N	J	F	I	E	O	Y	W	T	E	L	L	O
E	I	R	O	N	M	A	N	P	A	H	N	I	N	R
R	F	K	K	A	E	M	N	S	R	K	A	E	B	M
I	R	L	E	X	L	U	T	H	O	R	M	B	A	E
N	A	M	R	E	D	I	P	S	C	X	O	R	T	B
E	G	T	I	R	C	E	I	H	M	R	W	O	M	N
X	A	U	E	F	E	L	I	N	M	O	T	W	A	S
I	I	L	W	O	N	D	E	R	W	O	M	A	N	U
K	L	U	H	E	L	B	I	D	E	R	C	N	I	D
A	R	E	C	E	U	I	H	C	D	W	N	L	N	I
X	A	I	A	Y	A	A	O	E	P	M	H	L	A	L

TRUE LIFE COMIX (p. 99)
Semaphore: One day this will be worth a lot of money!

THE FORTU-NA-TOR (p. 106)

HONOR ROLL, OR NOT? (p. 114)

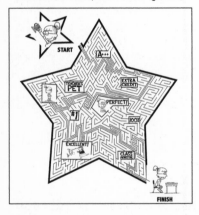

PERFECT PARTNERS (p. 138)

SAVED BY THE BELL (p. 109)

N	G	Y	A	T	E	I	R	H	G	S	I	C	L	O
O	N	R	L	J	T	I	O	N	E	C	G	N	L	T
U	I	E	Q	K	O	C	I	P	E	D	F	W	A	L
P	D	T	I	H	K	T	H	S	N	F	N	P	B	E
X	A	T	C	E	N	X	K	A	Q	R	D	V	K	E
L	E	O	Y	I	P	A	B	Q	E	A	O	I	C	B
L	L	P	A	E	T	I	M	P	N	K	M	D	I	S
A	R	P	T	I	V	M	A	C	M	R	P	E	K	I
B	E	U	N	A	T	P	I	N	U	J	J	O	R	R
E	G	U	E	L	N	H	P	O	V	K	G	F	E	F
S	H	S	L	O	G	S	G	N	I	T	C	A	A	N
A	C	L	O	G	N	O	P	G	N	I	P	M	D	I
B	A	H	A	E	T	A	R	A	K	W	W	E	I	A
B	C	L	L	A	B	T	E	K	S	A	B	S	N	B
S	T	R	N	B	O	B	A	Q	M	L	Z	A	G	C

TRIVIA TEST! (pp. 120–121)
1. (c) Mr. Staples
2. (d) Gina
3. (b) Cheez Doodles
4. (c) Spitsy
5. (b) figure skates

COMIX U CREATE (p. 123)
Semaphore: This is suspenseful!

NATE WRIGHT PRESENTS (p. 125)

D	R	E	U	G	F	N	T	B
G	B	U	E	T	N	R	D	F
T	F	N	B	R	D	E	U	G
E	N	D	T	B	R	F	G	U
R	T	G	D	F	U	B	N	E
F	U	B	N	E	G	D	R	T
U	E	F	R	D	T	G	B	N
B	D	T	G	N	E	U	F	R
N	G	R	F	U	B	T	E	D

THE JOKE'S ON YOU! (pp. 126–127)
Q: What do monsters read every day?
A: Their horrorscope!
Q: Why can't you play cards in the jungle?
A: Because there are too many cheetahs!

PET PARADISE (p. 141)

```
G N O T G B K C T S W S L W H
Y Y T K H J H T A U N O T L S
F E R R E T Y L E A R U U R I
P Q J G M L A C K E B T E E F
A C Z O D M Y E U Y K T L L D
R G I P A E N I U G S A I E L
R C T N T T J M D M G Z R X O
O S D E I H M H A S A Z O A G
T E A U B O O H Y R A N A C P
R N Y N B T U R G E R B I L
K Z T D A F S D S T X F G V X
Y G K M R U E Q T E F T V O I
X I K D Z G I A U D L D F D
Q S H E T W K I U A H B R Z T
Y N O P W X M X S V U A O X X
```

MUSICAL MADNESS (p. 153)

```
M E N P U A T P L O R A
I L U R S O N T S A T R
O T R U M P E T T N U R
U G E L G N A I R T B E
O V E N I R U O B M A T
L T X R O G H N A O C U
O H A R P H I B S N Y L
C L O L C L P A S U M F
C V E N O B M O R T B Y
I Y E I A I E L X A A C
P R V A M I V G E A L T
F D R U M S P T S S S B
```

EXTRA CREDIT (p. 165)
Semaphore: Does Mrs. Godfrey take her job too seriously? You decide!

SUPER SPOFF (p. 167)

```
G O G L S Z L U E C A O F L
R E M A L L L H R Y L L D T
D E H R T A A F U E O P K L
E R O H D E B A R O L E S A
G A L F E H T E R U T P A C
M U R R H N O H G P U H F T
O Q U E B T O C E D B A A E
O S E E A C F T O R O B A M
A R H Z K T G O N R B D E D
H U A A G A C E I E A U D
G O Y T G E L S R S M Y L T
E F N A C E F P R E F D R L
D U E G R E V O R D E R A H
Z F G E V S H H S U D L S B
```

DID YOU KNOW? (pp. 142–143)
The mid-ocean ridge is the largest mountain range in the world and it is underwater.
There are about one hundred trillion cells in the human body.
The bulldog bat from South America eats fish.

WHO'S IN LOVE? (p. 147)

G	N	A	J
J	A	N	G
N	J	G	A
A	G	J	N

SCHOOL RULES (p. 159)

Crossword answers: WOODSHOP, SPELLING, SPANISH, ART, DRAMA, COMPUTER, RECESS, HEALTH, GYM, MATH, SCIENCE, PRINCIPAL, etc.

NO LESSON PLAN! (p. 171)

S	C	H	R
H	R	C	S
R	H	S	C
C	S	R	H

LIFE IS CRAZY (pp. 174–175)
Semaphores: Does Nate have a twin? Coach John is insane. Funny stuff!

COMIX CRUSH (p. 179)
Semaphore: Uh-oh!

SHOWDOWN! (p. 181)

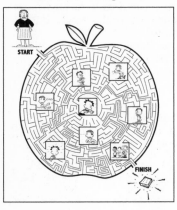

OUTBURSTS! (pp. 184–185)
Semaphores: Goody Two-shoes
She looks mad!
Heads up!

NATE IQ TEST (pp. 188-190)
1.   (d) Doctor Cesspool
2.   (c) Fleeceball
3.   (c) Mr. Eustis
4.   (e) None of the above
Extra Credit (c) Ben Franklin
Extra Extra Credit (Semaphore:)
What test has only four questions?
(Teddy code): This one, genius!

MASTERMIND (p. 191)
Semaphore: Wow! You're a brainiac!

LAUGH-A-MINUTE (pp. 192–193)
Semaphores: Why is Nate smiling?
Big sisters are annoying!
Gina is ready to bite Nate's head off!

ATHLETE OF THE YEAR (p. 197)

V	Y	S	F	B	D	T	R	H
F	R	H	T	S	Y	D	V	B
D	B	T	H	V	R	Y	S	F
H	T	F	R	D	V	S	B	Y
B	D	Y	S	F	H	R	T	V
R	S	V	B	Y	T	F	H	D
S	V	D	Y	T	B	H	F	R
Y	F	R	V	H	S	B	D	T
T	H	B	D	R	F	V	Y	S

SHOUT IT OUT! (pp. 200–201)
Semaphores: Baby pictures are so
embarrassing.
Noogie convention!
Baa! What's up with Nate?

BIG NATE ON A ROLL IS NEXT!

TURN THE PAGE FOR A SNEAK PEEK!

NATE WRIGHT: SUPER SCOUT!

I'll be honest: I used to think scouting was for dorks. But that was before Francis and Teddy convinced me to join their Timber Scout troop. **NOW** I know the truth: *SCOUTS ROCK!* For one thing, you get to wear an awesome uniform!

I LOVE your beret!

Plus, being a scout means going on overnight camping trips. That's always a blast, except for the time Dad came along as a parent volunteer. (Two words: **NEVER AGAIN!**)

Look at the squirrel, kids!

Dad, that's a SKUNK!

Scouting isn't free, though, so sometimes we do fund-raisers to earn money for our troop. Here's the

problem: when you're trying to sell butt-ugly wall hangings of kittens and unicorns, you get a lot of doors slammed in your face.

You want me to buy **THAT**?

But it'll be worth it. Because guess what the grand prize is for the scout who raises the most money? (*HINT*: my old one is at the bottom of a swamp.)

It won't be easy. My main competitor, who's good at **EVERYTHING**, is probably a great salesman. I'll add that to the list of things I hate about him.

mystery rival

Want to know what happens? Here's how to find out:

Read **BIG NATE ON A ROLL**!

MY GREATEST ADVENTURE YET!

"Big Nate is funny, big time."
—Jeff Kinney, author of Diary of a Wimpy Kid

BIG NATE
ON A ROLL

Lincoln Peirce

Lincoln Peirce

is a cartoonist/writer and the author of the *New York Times* bestsellers *Big Nate: In a Class by Himself, Big Nate Strikes Again,* and the collections *Big Nate: From the Top* and *Big Nate: Out Loud.* He is also the creator of the comic strip *Big Nate.* It appears in two hundred and fifty U.S. newspapers and online daily at www.bignate.com. *Big Nate* was selected for *Horn Book Magazine*'s Fanfare List of Best Books of 2010 and BarnesandNoble.com's Top Ten. Also, *Big Nate* will be published in sixteen countries, including Brazil, Canada, China, the Czech Republic, France, Germany, Greece, Holland, Indonesia, Israel, Italy, Japan, Portugal, Spain, Taiwan, and Turkey, and will be translated into eighteen languages.

Check out Big Nate Island at www.poptropica.com. And link to www.bignatebooks.com for games, blogs, and more information about *Big Nate Boredom Buster* and the author, who lives with his wife and two children in Portland, Maine.

BIG NATE ON A ROLL AND
BIG NATE GOES FOR BROKE
ARE IN YOUR FUTURE!